92 /
BAN
c.1 Conley, Kevin
    Benjamin Banneker

92 /
BAN
c.1 Conley, Kevin
    Benjamin Banneker

16.00

DATE DUE	BORROWER'S NAME
SEP. 1 1991	Mason Simmons 308
	Alex Hernandez 309
SEP. 2 1991 10-3-91	Mason Simmons 308
NOV. 20 1991	Beth Liggett 206

BENJAMIN BANNEKER

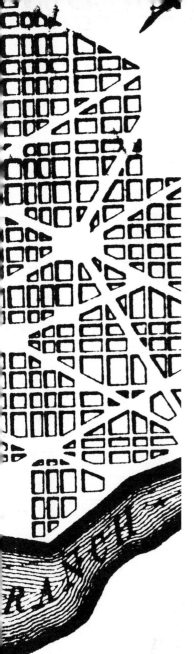

BENJAMIN BANNEKER

❦

Kevin Conley

Senior Consulting Editor
Nathan Irvin Huggins
Director
W.E.B. Du Bois Institute for Afro-American Research
Harvard University

CHELSEA HOUSE PUBLISHERS
New York   Philadelphia

Chelsea House Publishers
Editor-in-Chief Nancy Toff
Executive Editor Remmel T. Nunn
Managing Editor Karyn Gullen Browne
Copy Chief Juliann Barbato
Picture Editor Adrian G. Allen
Art Director Maria Epes
Manufacturing Manager Gerald Levine

Black Americans of Achievement
Senior Editor Richard Rennert

Staff for BENJAMIN BANNEKER
Assistant Editor Heather Lewis
Deputy Copy Chief Nicole Bowen
Editorial Assistant Navorn Johnson
Picture Researcher Patricia Burns
Assistant Art Director Loraine Machlin
Designer Ghila Krajzman
Production Coordinator Joseph Romano
Cover Illustration Alan Nahigian

3   5   7   9   8   6   4

Library of Congress Cataloging-in-Publication Data
Conley, Kevin.
    Benjamin Banneker / Kevin Conley.
        p.   cm.
    Bibliography: p.
    Includes index.
    Summary: A biography of the eighteenth-century black tobacco
farmer who taught himself mathematics, astronomy, and clock-
making; became famous for his almanacs; and assisted in the original
survey of Washington, D.C.
    ISBN 1-55546-573-0
        0-7910-0231-4 (pbk.)
    1. Banneker, Benjamin, 1731–1806—Juvenile literature.
2. Astronomers—United States—Juvenile literature. 3. Afro-
Americans—United States—Biography—Juvenile literature.
[1. Banneker, Benjamin, 1731–1806. 2. Astronomers. 3. Afro-
Americans—Biography.] I. Title.
QB36.B22C66 1990
509.2—dc20   89-34598
[B]   CIP
[92]   AC

CONTENTS

———— ❦ ————

BLACK AMERICANS OF ACHIEVEMENT

RALPH ABERNATHY
civil rights leader

MUHAMMAD ALI
heavyweight champion

RICHARD ALLEN
religious leader and social activist

LOUIS ARMSTRONG
musician

ARTHUR ASHE
tennis great

JOSEPHINE BAKER
entertainer

JAMES BALDWIN
author

BENJAMIN BANNEKER
scientist and mathematician

AMIRI BARAKA
poet and playwright

COUNT BASIE
bandleader and composer

ROMARE BEARDEN
artist

JAMES BECKWOURTH
frontiersman

MARY MCLEOD BETHUNE
educator

BLANCHE BRUCE
politician

RALPH BUNCHE
diplomat

GEORGE WASHINGTON CARVER
botanist

CHARLES CHESNUTT
author

BILL COSBY
entertainer

PAUL CUFFE
merchant and abolitionist

FATHER DIVINE
religious leader

FREDERICK DOUGLASS
abolitionist editor

CHARLES DREW
physician

W.E.B. DU BOIS
scholar and activist

PAUL LAURENCE DUNBAR
poet

KATHERINE DUNHAM
dancer and choreographer

MARIAN WRIGHT EDELMAN
civil rights leader and lawyer

DUKE ELLINGTON
bandleader and composer

RALPH ELLISON
author

JULIUS ERVING
basketball great

JAMES FARMER
civil rights leader

ELLA FITZGERALD
singer

MARCUS GARVEY
black-nationalist leader

DIZZY GILLESPIE
musician

PRINCE HALL
social reformer

W. C. HANDY
father of the blues

WILLIAM HASTIE
educator and politician

MATTHEW HENSON
explorer

CHESTER HIMES
author

BILLIE HOLIDAY
singer

JOHN HOPE
educator

LENA HORNE
entertainer

LANGSTON HUGHES
poet

ZORA NEALE HURSTON
author

JESSE JACKSON
civil rights leader and politician

JACK JOHNSON
heavyweight champion

JAMES WELDON JOHNSON
author

SCOTT JOPLIN
composer

BARBARA JORDAN
politician

MARTIN LUTHER KING, JR.
civil rights leader

ALAIN LOCKE
scholar and educator

JOE LOUIS
heavyweight champion

RONALD MCNAIR
astronaut

MALCOLM X
militant black leader

THURGOOD MARSHALL
Supreme Court justice

ELIJAH MUHAMMAD
religious leader

JESSE OWENS
champion athlete

CHARLIE PARKER
musician

GORDON PARKS
photographer

SIDNEY POITIER
actor

ADAM CLAYTON POWELL, JR.
political leader

LEONTYNE PRICE
opera singer

A. PHILIP RANDOLPH
labor leader

PAUL ROBESON
singer and actor

JACKIE ROBINSON
baseball great

BILL RUSSELL
basketball great

JOHN RUSSWURM
publisher

SOJOURNER TRUTH
antislavery activist

HARRIET TUBMAN
antislavery activist

NAT TURNER
slave revolt leader

DENMARK VESEY
slave revolt leader

MADAME C. J. WALKER
entrepreneur

BOOKER T. WASHINGTON
educator

HAROLD WASHINGTON
politician

WALTER WHITE
civil rights leader and author

RICHARD WRIGHT
author

ON
ACHIEVEMENT

————— ❧ —————

Coretta Scott King

Before you begin this book, I hope you will ask yourself what the word *excellence* means to you. I think that it's a question we should all ask and keep asking as we grow older and change. Because the truest answer to it should never change. When you think of excellence, perhaps you think of success at work; or of becoming wealthy; or meeting the right person, getting married, and having a good family life.

Those important goals are worth striving for, but there is a better way to look at excellence. As Martin Luther King, Jr., said in one of his last sermons, "I want you to be first in love. I want you to be first in moral excellence. I want you to be first in generosity. If you want to be important, wonderful. If you want to be great, wonderful. But recognize that he who is greatest among you shall be your servant."

My husband, Martin Luther King, Jr., knew that the true meaning of achievement is service. When I met him, in 1952, he was already ordained as a Baptist preacher and was working toward a doctoral degree at Boston University. I was studying at the New England Conservatory and dreamed of accomplishments in music. We married a year later, and after I graduated the following year we moved to Montgomery, Alabama. We didn't know it then, but our notions of achievement were about to undergo a dramatic change.

You may have read or heard about what happened next. What began with the boycott of a local bus line grew into a national movement, and by the time he was assassinated in 1968 my husband had fashioned a black movement powerful enough to shatter forever the practice of racial segregation. What you may not have read about is where he got his method for resisting injustice without compromising his religious beliefs.

He adopted the strategy of nonviolence from a man of a different race, who lived in a distant country, and even practiced a different religion. The man was Mahatma Gandhi, the great leader of India, who devoted his life to serving humanity in the spirit of love and nonviolence. It was in these principles that Martin discovered his method for social reform. More than anything else, those two principles were the key to his achievements.

This book is about black Americans who served society through the excellence of their achievements. It forms a part of the rich history of black men and women in America—a history of stunning accomplishments in every field of human endeavor, from literature and art to science, industry, education, diplomacy, athletics, jurisprudence, even polar exploration.

Not all of the people in this history had the same ideals, but I think you will find something that all of them have in common. Like Martin Luther King, Jr., they all decided to become "drum majors" and serve humanity. In that principle—whether it was expressed in books, inventions, or song—they found something outside themselves to use as a goal and a guide. Something that showed them a way to serve others, instead of living only for themselves.

Reading the stories of these courageous men and women not only helps us discover the principles that we will use to guide our own lives but also teaches us about our black heritage and about America itself. It is crucial for us to know the heroes and heroines of our history and to realize that the price we paid in our struggle for equality in America was dear. But we must also understand that we have gotten as far as we have partly because America's democratic system and ideals made it possible.

We are still struggling with racism and prejudice. But the great men and women in this series are a tribute to the spirit of our democratic ideals and the system in which they have flourished. And that makes their stories special and worth knowing.

BENJAMIN BANNEKER

---------------- 1 ----------------

"TO CALCULATE
A COMMON
ALMANACK"

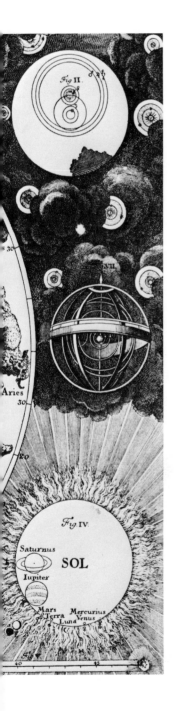

T HE U.S. CONSTITUTION was ratified on June 21, 1788, with the aim of protecting the natural rights of all Americans. In establishing a national government and providing the principles under which it was supposed to operate, the Constitution called for numerous checks and balances and a separation of powers "to form a more perfect Union." Yet the immediate implementation in nine states of "the supreme Law of the Land" failed to safeguard the personal liberties of free blacks such as Benjamin Banneker.

In a nation in which the majority of blacks were enslaved by whites, free blacks in the late 18th century were expected at all times to carry official papers that certified their status. They faced other legal restraints as well. They were not allowed to testify

In the fall of 1788, Banneker's newfound interest in astronomy prompted him to calculate a set of ephemerides—the positions of celestial bodies for each day of the year. His observations of the heavens were based on the astronomical theories of the scientists Johannes Kepler, Isaac Newton, and, first and foremost, the 16th-century astronomer Nicolaus Copernicus, who postulated that the sun was at the center of the solar system. This 18th-century engraving contrasts the Copernican system (center) with the Ptolemaic system, in which the sun orbited the earth (figs. I, II, and III).

11

against whites in some states, nor were they permitted to serve on a jury or be tried by one. On occasion, severe restrictions were placed on when and where they could travel, the violation of which could result in a heavy fine.

Although free blacks were certainly better off than slaves, they remained outcasts caught between two worlds—the white population and the slave society—largely because their very existence threatened the white majority. Maintaining that free blacks made slaves uneasy with their own limited status and were the leading cause of slave insurrections, whites were apt to treat the former with scorn. To avoid such hostile encounters, many free blacks chose to live in isolation.

Banneker was one of them. In the fall of 1788, he was still tending a remote tobacco plantation in central Maryland, much as he had been doing for the past 30 years. The tract of land measured 100 acres and was just small enough for the 57-year-old farmer to manage by himself. In fact, if his property had been any larger, he would not have had enough free time to engage in other activities that he so obviously enjoyed: reading books and newspapers, figuring out mathematical puzzles, and playing his flute or violin.

Banneker's modest farm was located along the upper Patapsco River, not far from Chesapeake Bay and just a mile away from Ellicott Mills, where there lived the prosperous owners of a huge flour mill. One of the most industrious members of this prominent family was George Ellicott, a 28-year-old surveyor. He and Banneker, a much older man whose grandfather and father had been slaves, seemed an unlikely pair. Nevertheless, they shared a deep love of science, and the friendship that they had established in 1778 was still going strong 10 years later.

By that time, Ellicott realized that his steadily increasing business concerns were preventing him

George Ellicott, a young surveyor in Maryland who lived near Banneker, "was in the habit of giving gratuitous lessons on astronomy," his daughter said, "to any of the inhabitants of the village who wished to hear him." In 1788, Ellicott lent Banneker the books and scientific equipment that piqued his interest in astronomy.

James Ferguson, an 18th-century Scottish astronomer, was widely known for writing books that attempted to make complex scientific principles more accessible to the general public. Banneker relied heavily on two of Ferguson's works, An Easy Introduction to Astronomy and Astronomy Explained Upon Sir Isaac Newton's Principles, in learning about astronomy.

from pursuing his hobby as an amateur astronomer. Accordingly, he gathered the various instruments he used to study the heavens and carried them to Banneker's cabin. Among the items Ellicott brought for his friend were a pedestal telescope and a set of drafting instruments to help him locate the position of the stars.

Ellicott also brought along four books. Two of the volumes were by James Ferguson, a popular lecturer on astronomy: An Easy Introduction to Astronomy and Astronomy Explained Upon Sir Isaac Newton's Principles, a more rigorous text. The other books were Charles Leadbetter's A Compleat System of Astronomy, which was more advanced than Ferguson's works, and *Mayer's Tables*, which included a group of ephemerides—tables that indicate the position of a celestial body for each day of the year.

Ellicott reminded himself to pass on to Banneker one more item, a sturdy table, because an astronomer requires an even surface for his telescope. The small, wobbly table in Banneker's cabin was the same one his father had made a long time ago, and it had become extremely worn after years of use. A large work area would serve Banneker much better.

A few days later, Ellicott sent his friend a huge oak table. Although it was scarred and scratched, it perfectly suited Banneker's purpose. It had a drawer, two drop leaves, and a surface large enough to hold his new books, telescope, and drafting instruments. He pushed the table against a wall and positioned it under his window so he could observe the night sky. Then he was ready to plunge into each book's dizzying sea of figures and begin his studies in earnest.

Ellicott had promised to visit Banneker in the not-too-distant future and explain the basic principles of astronomy. But an impatient Banneker was unwilling to wait for his friend's return. He looked through the telescope and observed the stars. He opened up Ferguson's *An Easy Introduction to Astronomy* and quickly mastered its contents. After a few nights, he had familiarized himself with the constellations, identifying them from the information given in the books.

A few weeks later, Banneker attempted to make a mathematical drawing of a solar eclipse. A total solar eclipse, in which the sun, moon, and earth are lined up in such a way that all of the sun (except for the corona, the outermost part of the sun's atmosphere) is obscured from the earth by the moon, occurs about once every 360 years. Partial eclipses occur much more often—at least once a month.

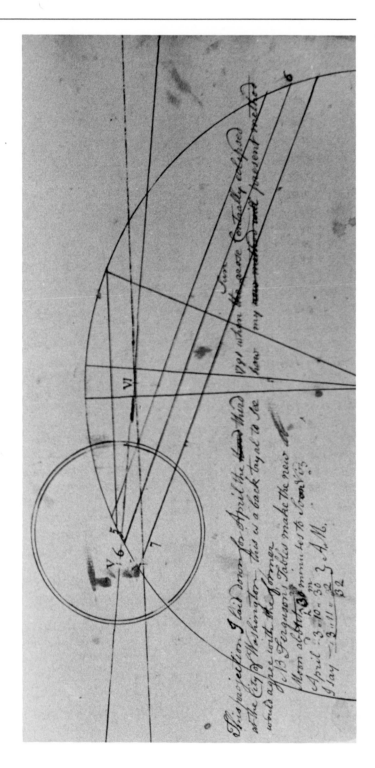

Banneker's diagram of an eclipse on April 3, 1791, which he drew with the help of a compass and ruler. Making a projection such as this one was an important step in putting together an almanac.

Figuring out precisely when a solar eclipse is going to occur is essentially a geometry problem. First, the paths of the sun and the moon have to be charted. Next, the point where they are in alignment with the earth must be identified.

Using Ferguson's *Astronomy Explained Upon Sir Isaac Newton's Principles* and Leadbetter's *A Compleat System of Astronomy* to guide him, Banneker employed a compass and a ruler to construct a drawing of the eclipse, which is known as a projection. Although the scientific work was complicated, meticulous attention came naturally to Banneker. When he had completed the projection, he checked it over many times. Finally, he was satisfied with the accuracy of his drawing and put it away, looking forward to the day when Ellicott would be ready to review his work.

George Ellicott gave Banneker this table in the late 1780s so he would have a large surface on which to carry out his scientific work. Throughout the rest of his life, Banneker spent many hours at this drop-leaf table, looking at the stars through a telescope and writing down his observations.

A man of many talents, Benjamin Franklin (right) first published Poor Richard's Almanack *(opposite) in 1732. Perhaps the most popular almanac ever produced, it served as a model for many similar publications.*

The day was slow in coming, however. Business matters prevented Ellicott from meeting with Banneker. At last, Banneker was unable to wait any longer. He made a copy of his scientific work and sent it with a letter to his mentor at Ellicott Mills. But he received no response and soon learned that business was keeping Ellicott away from home.

It was weeks before Ellicott returned from his trip. When he found Banneker's letter with the enclosed

Poor Richard, 1733.

A N

Almanack

For the Year of Chrift

1733,

Being the Firft after LEAP YEAR:

And makes fince the Creation	**Years**
By the Account of the Eaftern Greeks	7241
By the Latin Church, when ☉ ent. ♈	6932
By the Computation of *W. W.*	5742
By the *Roman* Chronology	5682
By the *Jewifh Rabbies*	5494

Wherein is contained

The Lunations,. Eclipfes, Judgment of the Weather, Spring Tides, Planets Motions & mutual Afpects, Sun and Moon's Rifing and Setting. Length of Days. Time of High Water,. Fairs, Courts, and obfervable Days Fitted to the Latitude of Forty Degrees and a Meridian of Five Hours Weft from *London,* but may without fenfible Error ferve all the adjacent Places, even from *Newfoundland* to *South Carolina,*

By *RICHARD SAUNDERS,* Philom.

PHILADELPHIA.
Printed and fold by *B. FRANKLIN,* at the New Printing.Office ne·· the Market.

projection, he immediately remembered his promise to instruct Banneker in the basic principles of astronomy. But the projection indicated that his friend needed little tutoring. There was only one small error in Banneker's calculation, which Ellicott explained in a letter of congratulations.

Nevertheless, Banneker was embarrassed by his error and returned to the projection to discover the source of his miscalculation. He decided that a discrepancy in the two texts he used was the reason for his mistake and sent a letter of explanation to Ellicott. In actuality, both books were accurate. Leadbetter's book described how to plot an eclipse from the earth, and Ferguson's volume assumed that the astronomer was standing on the sun. Banneker's error had in fact stemmed from his using two texts that were incompatible.

"Now Sir," Banneker wrote in his second letter to Ellicott, "if I can overcome this difficulty I Doubt not being able to Calculate a Common Almanack." Many self-taught astronomers of his era composed tables indicating the daily position of celestial bodies and published these charts in an almanac. In early America, where few printing presses were in operation and newspapers were not widespread, an almanac was the one book other than the Bible that was regarded as indispensable. Publishers throughout the new nation actively sought astronomers who could calculate the ephemerides for their local area.

An almanac was useful to people from all walks of life. It was where they obtained their yearly calendar and determined when holy days and festivals were celebrated. It assisted farmers by providing them with weather forecasts, a calendar of the different phases of the moon, and tables indicating planting and harvesting dates. It furnished sailors with a chart of the stars to help them plot their position on the seas. For those people who owned a watch or clock, it was their sole resource for accurately setting their timepiece.

In fact, for most people in 18th-century America who did not own a clock, an almanac was the only source they could consult if they wanted to find out the time of day. A standard feature in each almanac was a listing of the times of sunrise, noon, and sunset. Accordingly, almanacs were printed in greater numbers than any other texts in early America, and astronomers who calculated accurate ephemerides were in constant demand.

In the fall of 1789, Banneker completed the tables for his first almanac and arranged them in book format. To ensure the accuracy of his calculations, he carefully checked his work for errors. Then he sent the material to a printer in Baltimore, who showed little enthusiasm for the project. His second attempt at obtaining a publisher for his almanac resulted in failure as well. John Hayes, a former newspaper publisher and antislavery activist who had published several almanacs compiled by George Ellicott's cousin Major Andrew Ellicott, was the third recipient of Banneker's manuscript.

After a fair amount of time had passed, Banneker wrote to Hayes and asked for a verdict on his scientific work. When the amateur astronomer failed to receive a reply, he wrote again to the publisher. Hayes responded that he had sent Banneker's manuscript to Major Ellicott, who was in the process of assessing the accuracy of Banneker's figures.

Banneker promptly wrote to the major on May 6, 1790:

S^r// I have at the request of Several Gentlemen Calculated an Ephemeris for the year 1791 which I presented unto M^r. Hayes printer in Baltimore, and he received it in a very polite manner and told me that he would gladly print the Same provided the Calculations Came any ways near the truth, but to Satisfy himself in that he would Send it to philadelphia to be inspected by you and at the reception of an answer from you he Should know how to proceed and now S^r. I beg that you will not be too Severe upon me. . . . I hope that you will be kind enough to view with any eye of pitty as the Calculations was made more for the Sake of gratifying the Curiosity of the public, than for any view of profit, as I suppose it to be the first attempt of the kind that ever was made in America by a person of my Complection.

Maryland Baltimore County near Ellicott
     Lower Mills May the 6: 1790

I have at the request of Several Gentlemen, Calculated
an Ephemeris for the Year 1791 which I presented unto Mr
Hayes printer in Baltimore, and he received it in a very polite
manner and told me that he would gladly print the Same provided
the Calculations Came any ways near the truth, but to Satisfy him-
Self in that he would Send it to philadelphia to be inspected by you and
at the reception of an answer he Should know how to proceed
and now Sr I beg that you will not be too Severe upon me but as favourable
in giving your approbation as the nature of the Case will permit, knowing
well the difficulty that attends long Calculations and especially with
young beginners in Astronomy, but this I know that the greater and
most useful part of my Ephemeris is so near the truth that it needs
but little Correction, and as to that part that may be Somewhat deficient, I hope that you will be kind enough
to view with an eye of pitty as the Calculations was made more
for the Sake of gratifying the Curiosity of the public, than for any
view of profit, as I Suppose it to be the first attempt of the kind that
ever was made in America by a person of my Complection ——
I find by my Calculation there will be four Eclipses for the ensuing
year but I have not yet Settled their appearances, But am waiting for
an answer from your Honour to Mr Hayes in Baltimore.
So no more at present, but am Sr your very humble and most
          obedient Servt
                              B Banneker

In the spring of 1790, Banneker wrote this letter to Major Andrew Ellicott, a noted surveyor and almanac maker, in an attempt to gain his support for publishing an almanac the following year.

Despite Banneker's plea, Hayes elected not to publish the almanac. The amateur astronomer was told by the Baltimore printer that his firm had decided to print almanacs that contained only Major Ellicott's calculations. Unfortunately for Banneker, by the time he received word from Hayes that his manuscript would not be used, it was too late for him to interest someone else in publishing his work. His first opportunity to put out an almanac had been lost.

Nevertheless, Banneker had made an important contact in the publishing world—one that he soon put to good use. In 1792, a year after he was chosen to help survey the land that was to become the District of Columbia, Hayes helped him publish his first almanac. This book, along with subsequent editions, not only reached a large readership but also received the widespread support of antislavery activists, who read Banneker's text to legislative bodies in both the United States and abroad as part of their campaign to put an end to slavery and defeat the doctrine of white supremacy.

What began as a simple act of sharing between George Ellicott and Banneker ultimately became of great importance to the growing movement for black freedom in early America. Wherever abolitionists argued that blacks should be granted their full legal rights, the achievements they pointed to most often as proof that blacks deserved the same opportunities as whites were those of Benjamin Banneker, America's first black man of science. ◖◗

of Q:
Albion.

so her
profitab
eat Brit

IN

The falls

Henrico tow

MARY LAND
the Lord Baltemore Plantation
begun 1635,

Matwomient river

Patomak

Patuxunt River

Mary land

St Mary's

Checepiacke   200 miles

Elk river

The Bay of

Col Littletons Ile
The Easterne Shore or Leoma
land Squire Yeardly planta

Mataponyungo river

Myotin

Tockwogh river

Fets Island

Cingoto Ilo

Cape Iames

Lord Delawars Bay and Rive

Cape May

Egg bay

C V M.

Hudsons

2

NEW LANDS, LOST FREEDOMS

Benjamin BANNEKER WAS born on November 9, 1731, in what was then the British colony of Maryland. His grandmother Molly Welsh had settled in the area almost 50 years earlier, after a series of unusual events had taken place. While working as a dairymaid on an English cattle farm, located most likely in Wessex County, she tipped over a pail of milk during the course of her morning chores. Her employer accused her of taking the milk and had her arrested. According to the laws of 17th-century England, stealing was 1 of 300 felonies that were punishable by death.

There were, however, several ways to commute the sentence. One of them was for convicts such as Molly to ask to see the Bible (a procedure known as "calling for the book"). If the prisoner showed that he or she could read, the sentence would be reduced. In Molly's case, her ability to read saved her life.

It also sent Molly on her way to the colonies. On occasion, a convict who had been handed the death penalty was pardoned on the condition that he or she leave England and work in colonial America, where plantation owners were seeking cheap labor, black or white, to work on their farms. Molly agreed to such

A map showing the Virginia and Maryland colonies in the mid-17th century, around the time that the first of Banneker's ancestors came to the New World.

an offer, and her voyage overseas was soon set in motion by a sheriff who contacted a merchant with ties to the colonies. The merchant paid the costs of Molly's transatlantic passage, confident that he would recoup his investment upon their arrival in the New World by hiring out Molly as an indentured servant. Bound to work for another person for a specified amount of time (in the colonies the period was usually five to seven years), an indentured servant ranked

An engraving of an English dairy-maid. Banneker's maternal grandmother, Molly Welsh, was working on a farm in the 1600s when she was falsely accused of stealing milk. She was arrested by the authorities, who pardoned her on the condition that she leave England and settle in the American colonies.

between a free person and a slave. For the period of indenture the servant owed his or her employer complete allegiance.

Convicts and merchants were not the only people who made the arduous voyage to colonial America. Shipmasters scoured England for all sorts of people willing, in essence, to trade several years of their life for the price of passage to America. Farm laborers, craftsmen, house servants, carpenters, mechanics, and tutors were among those who agreed to travel to the New World.

The ships that crossed the Atlantic were small and cramped. Provisions were scanty, and the length of the journey was unpredictable; depending on the weather conditions, the voyage could take anywhere from 45 to 140 days. For the people who were being transported more or less as cargo to be sold upon their arrival, traveling conditions were particularly harsh. Moreover, the departures from England and the disembarkations in the colonies were subject to lengthy delays.

The ship carrying Molly reached the English province of Maryland in 1683. Maryland at that time prohibited the importation of convicts, so Molly either arrived on America's shores already bound to an employer, or else she was hidden among the craftspeople who came to the New World anxious to help America grow. She was indentured for seven years to the owner of a tobacco plantation located near the Patapsco River.

Molly's owner provided her with food, clothing, and shelter, and she in turn served him obediently. She had to remain within 10 miles of his property unless she had a pass that allowed her to travel greater distances. If she failed to comply with this restriction or committed any other offense, she would receive a whipping. Although Molly's living conditions were mild when compared with those faced by slaves, they nevertheless helped her understand what it felt like to be a slave.

Molly faced a difficult situation when she obtained her freedom in 1690. Early in Maryland's history, a law decreed that employers had to grant some sort of compensation to indentured servants who had fulfilled their obligations. When the provision first went into effect, those who were freed usually received a parcel of land to help them make a new start. But the law was soon changed, and by the time Molly Welsh finished serving her term, she was given her freedom and nothing else.

Molly managed to rent a small plot of land from a neighboring farmer in exchange for most of her proceeds from the following year's crop. She proved to be a hard worker. Laboring alone in the wilderness, clearing the land and planting tobacco, she set aside enough from her profits over the next few years to buy a small but promising patch of land near the Patapsco River.

But the going was difficult for Molly. Cooperative neighbors may have helped her out from time to time. For the most part, though, she worked in solitude. There is no record of what happened to Molly during her first few years on the farm except that within several summers after buying her property she had saved enough money to buy two slaves.

These slaves came from Africa to the New World by way of the torturous ocean journey known as the Middle Passage. Between 5 and 10 million Africans died on slave ships, where barbarous conditions were the norm. The ships were specifically designed for transporting as many slaves as possible, and the kidnapped Africans were locked in airless holds that provided each person with a space that was only 18 inches wide. During a typical voyage, a quarter to a third of the Africans died while crossing the Atlantic.

Once a day—when the weather permitted—the slaves were brought on deck. They were fed cornmeal scooped from a barrel and washed down with seawater. Then they were driven back into their dark hold. When the opportunity presented itself, many slaves jumped overboard to escape their agony—so many, in fact, that schools of sharks soon began to trail the ships.

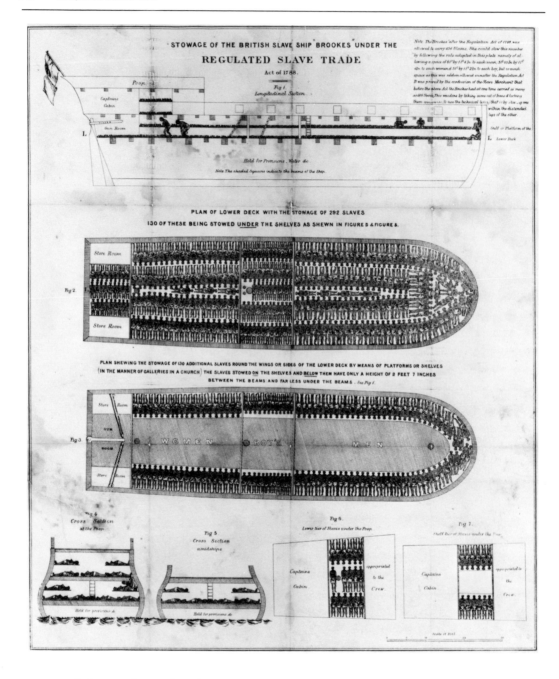

A diagram showing how slaves were shipped to the New World when the slave trade
was at its height. Banneker's father and maternal grandfather were among those who
were chained to other Africans in the airless hold of a slave ship.

Both of Molly's slaves managed to survive the Middle Passage in relatively good health. One of them, whose name is not known, was very strong, making him well suited for tackling the heavy tasks on Molly's tobacco farm: felling trees, plowing the land, and putting in long hours at harvesttime. The other man, named Bannaka, had a slight build and seemed averse to work. Molly asked him to handle the lighter chores.

As the months passed, Molly learned to communicate with the delicate Bannaka, who told her he was an African prince. His claim may have been true. Throughout the history of the slave trade it was common practice when rival African states were at war for one tribe to capture an opposing tribe's royal family and sell the members to European slave traders.

Bannaka certainly carried himself as if he were a nobleman. According to one of his descendants, Bannaka was "a man of bright intelligence, fine temper, with a very agreeable presence, dignified manners, and contemplative habits." He apparently retained a strong sense of pride in his African heritage. Whereas Molly's other slave converted to Christianity, Bannaka held on to his traditional beliefs. He also kept his African name, although it was altered in time to Banneky.

Within a few years, most likely in 1696, Molly freed both her slaves. Shortly thereafter, she married Banneky, an act that put them at great personal risk. Colonial laws governing interracial marriage had become increasingly rigid over the years. In 1681, a law had been passed in Maryland prohibiting ministers from marrying a black man and "a white woman servant freeborn." Three years later, another law was passed: A white woman who married a black man or had his child was considered to have relinquished her freedom. She then became a servant "to the use of the Minister of the Poor of the same Parish."

Several other factors made the newlyweds' hold on freedom even more tenuous. In all likelihood, neither Molly nor Banneky had written documentation of their having been freed. Moreover, Molly owned property at a time when women, regardless of their class or race, had almost no civil rights. The laws of the period regarded a woman as an object belonging to her father. (She became the property of her husband when she married.) So even if Molly had documented her freeing of Banneky, it is uncertain that her document would have stood up in a court of law.

Facing such grim prospects, Molly and Banneky withdrew from public view after their marriage. Their first child, Mary, was born in 1700. In the ensuing years, they had three more children: Katherine, Esther, and another girl whose name is no longer known.

The family concentrated on making its tobacco farm prosper. As more and more towns sprang up along the Patapsco, merchants from large English firms began to sail upriver and stop at each landing in search of tobacco. The merchants paid for the crop with tobacco notes, which soon became a form of currency in central Maryland, with each town's tobacco warehouse serving as an informal bank of credit and trade.

In the midst of this prosperous period, Banneky died, leaving Molly once again to manage the farm on her own. Even though she had four daughters to raise, she was up to the task. She had already left the land of her birth and endured years of forced labor. She had gotten used to overcoming formidable odds.

As Molly's daughters grew, they helped her farm the tobacco and bring the crop to the nearby landing, where it was sold to passing merchants. Mary, the eldest daughter, was especially helpful. Like her mother, she was strong in the fields and knew the secrets of cultivating tobacco. Therefore, it was a great relief to Molly that when Mary decided to marry in 1730 she did not leave the family farm.

Mary's husband was a free black named Robert, who promptly took her last name of Banneky as his own. A former slave who had been captured in northwest Africa and sold to a tobacco planter who lived near the Banneky farm, he received his freedom around the same time that he converted to Christianity and took the name Robert. In this last respect, he was unlike most slaves, whose African names were taken away and replaced by Christian names. Slaves were considered easier to manage when their past identity was destroyed.

The Banneky farm grew livelier again in late 1731, when Mary and Robert had their first child, a son they named Benjamin. They later had three daughters. The name of the eldest girl is no longer known; the other two girls were Minta and Molly. Their family name changed in time to Banneker.

As Robert's family grew, he and his wife began planning their own farm. They set aside some of the tobacco that they harvested from each year's crop, and they eventually used their savings to purchase a small, thickly wooded plot of land called Timber Poynt. It was located near Molly's farm. Robert cleared the 25 acres and planted wheat, corn, and, most importantly, tobacco. An expert planter, he watched over the tobacco daily.

By 1737, Robert had saved 7,000 pounds of tobacco—enough to buy an additional 100 acres on a tract of land called Stout. A deed was drawn up, a formal document transferring the property to the joint ownership of Robert Banneker and his son, Benjamin. Robert remembered how he had lost his freedom in Africa and was eager to protect his family's rights and give them a secure future by having a deed made.

The Africans who survived the torturous passage to the American colonies were unloaded in Georgia and Virginia and placed in dockside slave pens. They remained there for a few weeks so they could be cleaned and fattened before being sold into slavery.

Around the mouth of Chesapeake Bay, where the river emptied, the competition for tobacco farmland was fierce, and most of the men and women who had once been indentured servants were not able to afford the steep prices that such property commanded. Wealthy landowners presided over most of the area's tobacco plantations. But where the Bannekers lived, at the headwaters of the Chesapeake, there were few tobacco farms, which meant that Robert did not have to face a lot of stiff competition from other farmers. As a result, he was able to sell his harvest at reasonably good prices to the tobacco agents who made the journey upriver.

Before long, the Bannekers were earning a modest living and were as well off as most of the tobacco planters who lived along the upper reaches of the Patapsco River.

3

THE STRIKING CLOCK

BENJAMIN BANNEKER SPENT a good deal of his boyhood helping his father run the family farm. Maintaining a profitable farm in the 18th century was difficult enough under ordinary circumstances, but it was even harder for the colonies' relatively few free blacks, who were forced to shoulder most of the burdens by themselves. Whereas white farmers generally helped one another out when it came to performing major tasks such as barn raisings and harvesting crops, free blacks found themselves excluded from such communal efforts and had to go it alone.

Accordingly, Benjamin and his three younger sisters helped with the chores as soon as they were able. In the spring, they joined their parents in sowing the tobacco seeds from the previous year's plants in seedbeds located in the woods, where the soil conditions were best for young plants. Then, when the first shoots appeared, they transplanted the tobacco to the fields. This replanting marked a critical point in the growing cycle. Once transferred to the fields, the plants had to be guarded constantly. Insects could ruin a crop, and weeds could choke it. The Bannekers carefully tended the young plants, picking worms,

Shortly after Banneker was born in 1731, his parents purchased 25 acres of farmland called Timber Poynt. In 1737, they bought an additional 100 acres, known as Stout, near the Patapsco River and built a log cabin (much like the one shown in this engraving) that remained Banneker's home for the balance of his life.

aphids, and slugs from the shoots and weeding the earth with hoes.

In August, the hottest time of the year, came the harvesting, the final push to collect the tobacco leaves and ready them for transport. Benjamin and the others cut the plants, working fast enough to process their entire crop in just a few days. The plants were collected and hung in a tobacco house to dry. After five or six weeks, the drying leaves were still supple enough to be packaged.

Farmers in the 1700s packaged tobacco by compressing the leaves and securing them with barrel stays. Such a bundle was known as a hogshead. Maryland law stated that each hogshead had to be 48 inches high and have a diameter of 32 inches. Packaged in this uniform way, the amount of tobacco that a farmer had harvested could be easily determined.

The last step in tobacco farming was rolling the hogsheads along a series of "rolling roads." The roads

Banneker spent much of his boyhood helping his parents farm tobacco. Harvesting the tobacco leaves (below) and hanging them up to dry (opposite) were two of the many steps involved in the tobacco-growing process.

led to landings along the Patapsco River, where the crop was sold to a tobacco agent.

Tobacco farming consumed much of Benjamin's time throughout his youth. Yet it never held a very large place in his heart. Nor did the other chores on the family farm: feeding the animals, tending the vegetable garden, clearing the surrounding land. The only relief that he had from his labors was on the Sabbath, the traditional day of rest.

Whenever he had the chance, Benjamin took a break from his yard work and read. His grandmother Molly, whose ability to read had saved her life, gave him his first reading lesson from the only book she owned, a Bible she had ordered from England. She also taught her grandson how to write, and it became apparent from the outset that he had an exceptional mind.

Benjamin's chief interest, however, was arithmetic. He liked to formulate mathematical problems

In the 18th century, tobacco was transported in large bundles called hogsheads. Beasts of burden brought the crops to tobacco agents by pulling the packaged goods along specially established dirt trails known as rolling roads.

and figure out statistics, going so far as to break down tobacco farming into 36 distinct steps. He was also deeply interested in local history.

Before long, Benjamin had exhausted his grandmother's abilities as a teacher. The first to admit her limitations, she arranged for him to attend an integrated school that had recently been established in the area. Benjamin was one of several black pupils who attended the one-room school, and obtaining an education soon became the single most important object in his life. Jacob Hall, a classmate and lifelong friend of Banneker's, recalled that "all [Benjamin's] delight was to dive into his books."

Because school was held only during the winter months, Benjamin had to rely mostly on himself to advance his knowledge. He was clearly someone who could work hard and work alone—traits he shared with all the members of his family. And by the early 1750s his efforts began to pay extraordinary dividends.

When Banneker was 21 years old, he decided to build a clock, even though he had never seen the inside of such an object and did not know how one worked. After all, most of his acquaintances had little use for a timepiece. Time for most farmers was determined by when the sun came up and went down. A clock in 18th-century America was a rare thing, a wonder from Europe.

In colonial times, people regarded the orderly movement of the planets and the stars as comparable to the movements of a clock. They said that God himself worked like a clockmaker, timing the motion of the spheres, winding up the universe, and letting it run according to a precise plan. Philosophers liked to speak of clocks and their engineering as harbingers of what the human mind would soon achieve.

Few people in the 1700s kept constant track of time. In the Old World, church bells signaled the important moments of the day. In the New World, where churches were generally not as elaborate as their European counterparts and where most people lived on farms and plantations far from any settlements, churches rang their bells only for emergencies or celebrations. Indeed, the woods were so thick and the people so isolated in the tobacco country Banneker inhabited that only the most important events—the arrival of goods from Europe, the docking of a slave ship—were worth announcing. To do that, a cannon was fired.

In order to build a clock, Banneker needed to borrow a timepiece to serve as a model. Because clocks were hard to come by in colonial Maryland, that was no easy task. Yet he somehow managed to borrow a pocket watch. His next step was to examine the watch's interior and make drawings of its various components. He studied the motions of the second, minute, and hour wheels and noted how their actions meshed. He subsequently took some wood and carved a group of wheels that corresponded to the gears inside the pocket watch. However, he made these cogs much bigger, so that they were the same size as those inside the huge clocks he had seen delivered at nearby Elkridge Landing.

Banneker fashioned his clock almost entirely from wood. Then he added a final touch: a bell. When the clock was completed, it functioned accurately and chimed on the hour.

Word of Banneker's accomplishment soon spread throughout central Maryland. Decades later, when he had gone on to much greater accomplishments, people in the region still talked first and foremost about his clock. And what made the entire project even more astounding was that it kept accurate time for the rest of his life. "He acknowledged himself amply repaid for all his cares in its construction by the precision with which it marked the passing time," a neighbor said.

Banneker's clock was not the first timepiece to be constructed in the colonies. In other parts of North America, especially in the large cities, craftsmen such as David Rittenhouse of Philadelphia were fashioning handsome timepieces. Nevertheless, Banneker's clock demonstrated just how gifted a thinker he was.

On July 10, 1759, some six years after Banneker completed his clock, his father died. Because all three of his sisters had already married and moved away from Stout, running the farm became Banneker's responsibility. With the help of his mother, who was still strong and active in her sixties, he operated a successful farm. Records indicate that he owned two horses and a few cows, maintained several beehives

that his father had started, and kept a vegetable garden. Documents also show that in 1761 he registered a stray animal at the courthouse in Joppa, the county seat—an indication that Banneker, being a free black, felt he had to safeguard his property.

In 1763, Banneker made an important purchase. He bought his first book, a Bible, from a neighbor and entered the following inscription: "I bought this book of Honora Buchanan the 4th day of January 1763. B.B." He then added: "Benjamin Banneker was born November the 9th, in the year of the Lord God, 1731. Robert Banneker departed this life July the 10th, 1759."

Banneker first learned how to read and write from his grandmother Molly Welsh. She later enrolled him in a small local school, which he attended for only a few months each year because his parents needed his help on the family farm.

When Banneker was in his early twenties, he fashioned a striking clock out of wood. Similar in design to the timepiece shown here, his clock kept accurate time for more than 50 years.

Banneker also bought a flute and violin and learned to play both instruments. Neighbors recalled that he liked to sit on his porch and make music during the evening hours. For the most part, his was a lonely life. Working hard for most of the day, he had little chance to socialize. He knew some of the farmers in the surrounding area and conversed with the tradesmen who passed by every now and then. But he did not have many friends, and he never married. Being a free black seemed to cut him off from much of the world.

Yet Banneker did not remain completely isolated. His mathematical ability, which was well known throughout the area, prompted various neighbors to ask him to inspect their deeds and help them make mathematical calculations. Some neighbors even came to his cabin just to see his remarkable clock. He treated them very cordially but did not become close with them.

Banneker continued to lead the humble existence of a tobacco planter until he was 40 years old. Then a family named Ellicott moved near his farm, and their arrival completely changed Banneker's life. ◀◊▶

4

THE ELLICOTTS ARRIVE

T HE ELLICOTTS WERE an enterprising family that in 1771 took up residence in a treacherous valley on the Patapsco River less than a mile from Banneker's farm. They first left England for the New World in the early 1700s, when hard times hit their wool manufacturing business and they decided to try their luck in the colonies. Andrew Ellicott arrived in the colony of Pennsylvania with his son, Andrew II, who soon married a local woman named Ann Bye. They had five sons.

By the time Andrew II died in 1741, the family had little money left. Samuel Armitage, Andrew's business associate, became the boys' guardian and found apprentice work for them. The eldest Ellicott, Joseph, was employed at a gristmill, where he helped repair milling machinery. When his apprenticeship came to an end, he was commissioned by Armitage to construct a gristmill in Bucks County. Joseph did so with the help of his four brothers.

The mill soon became a success, and life for the Ellicotts began to take on a fairy-tale quality. In 1766, Joseph found out that a great-grandfather in Ireland had left him a valuable estate. Joseph sold the estate,

In 1771, a large tract of land along the Patapsco River in Maryland became the site of Ellicott Mills, a gristmill that was subsequently surrounded by a bustling community. Today, the town is known as Ellicott City and boasts a population of more than 20,000.

47

giving himself and his brothers the means to finance their own milling operation.

In search of the best place to launch their business, the Ellicotts looked for a river in which the current was strong enough to power a mill. They also sought a growing market for milling. Central Maryland offered promising signs, especially the region around Baltimore, whose recent surge in population had caused it to replace Joppa, a dwindling tobacco community, as the county seat. The Ellicotts found a promising spot on the Patapsco River 10 miles away from Baltimore and acquired 700 acres along the west riverbank.

Baltimore had grown during the French and Indian War, which began in 1754. Because the town

Baltimore, situated about 10 miles from Banneker's home, became one of Maryland's most heavily populated towns in the mid-1700s. Many colonists flocked to the town during the French and Indian War because Fort McHenry (left) offered them shelter; they remained there after the fighting ended because Baltimore's harbor offered them excellent commercial opportunities.

boasted a fort, a large number of colonists went there to seek shelter. When the war ended, many of the people remained, thereby making Baltimore one of the most heavily populated spots in Maryland. The Ellicotts looked to supply the growing town with flour and to take advantage of the local shipping routes, which had access to Chesapeake Bay and the Atlantic and allowed for the easy export of goods to Europe.

In 1771, two of the Ellicott brothers, John and Andrew III, arrived with a large work crew at their newly acquired site along the Patapsco River. They set up a shanty for their lodgings and then went to work, eventually building a mill that measured 100 feet long and 36 feet wide. Ellicott's Lower Mills stood one and a half stories high and was made entirely of stone. It featured five huge pairs of millstones that were used to ground the grain into flour. The Ellicotts expected to grind large quantities of grain in the mill, so they made its entrance large enough to accommodate a horse and wagon.

The farmers in the region, who were primarily tobacco growers, wondered where these ambitious men were going to get grain for their mill; all of the grain that was grown in the region was earmarked for family use. But the Ellicotts had addressed that problem, too. Their mill did not open until 1774, but when it did, the Ellicotts processed wheat, corn, and rye that they grew on their own land and sold the various flours in Baltimore. Their neighbors soon realized that if they produced crops other than tobacco and brought them to the mill for grinding, they could turn a handsome profit as well.

Because all of this happened so close to Banneker's property, he often made his way to Ellicott Mills. He was especially intrigued by the mill and asked the

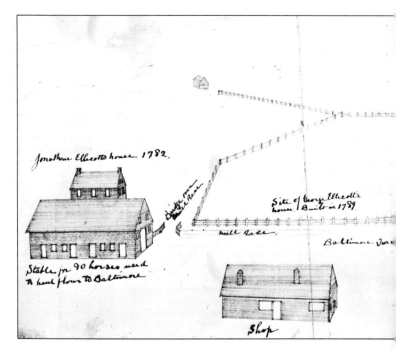

workers how it operated. Machinery carried the grain up to the top of the structure and dumped it onto the millstones. Once the grain was crushed into flour, other machines conveyed it to a packaging area, where the flour was poured into barrels. Machines also placed the barrels on wagons that transported the flour to Baltimore.

Banneker must have noticed that the Ellicotts, who were obviously wealthy and employed a lot of help, had seen to it that the construction work and the operation of the mill were performed without the use of slaves. Throughout the colonies, slavery was the cheapest source of labor. It was far less expensive to import a black from Africa and make him a slave than it was to raise a child and have him work. By 1770, nearly half of all the white families in the Chesapeake area owned at least one slave.

The Ellicotts, however, shunned this practice. In an era when the rights of blacks, women, and Native Americans were largely ignored, they maintained that

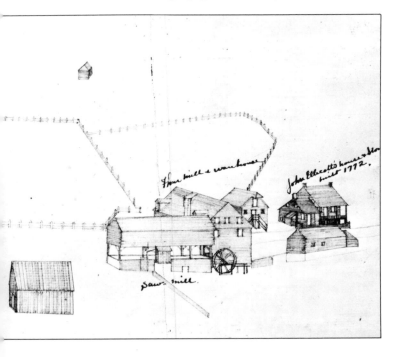

Ellicott's Lower Mills, as drawn by George Ellicott in 1782. The turnpike to Baltimore that he helped survey ran directly through the heart of this growing community.

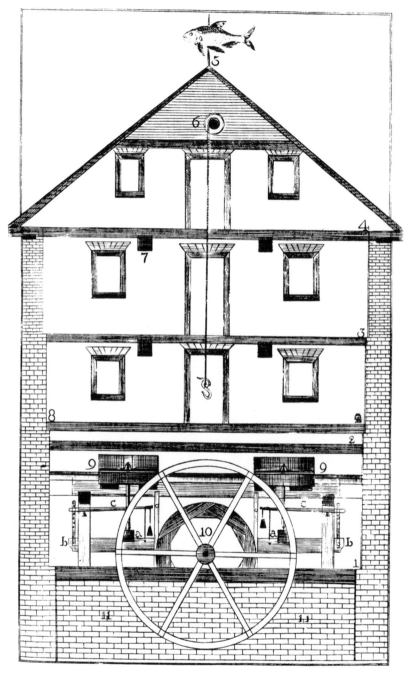

The exterior of a mill house constructed by the Ellicotts. Water from the Patapsco River turned the big wheel and powered the mill.

all people should be treated with equal respect. Whereas most churches viewed slavery as an acceptable practice, the Ellicotts belonged to the Society of Friends, a religious body of Christians (also known as Quakers) that called for the abolition of slavery in the New World.

George Fox, an English preacher, founded the Society of Friends in the 17th century. He emphasized the inner life extolled by Jesus Christ and said there was "that of God in every man" which communicated with each person through an "inner light." Because God resides in every person's soul, Fox reasoned, all people must be equal. Moreover, they did not need a formal church structure to act as an intermediary between themselves and God. Their religious services, known as Quaker meetings, did not have any rituals. Quiet contemplation was the norm, although

The interior of the Ellicotts' automated mill house. Its complex machinery indicated to Banneker that the Ellicotts shared his interest in mathematics and mechanics.

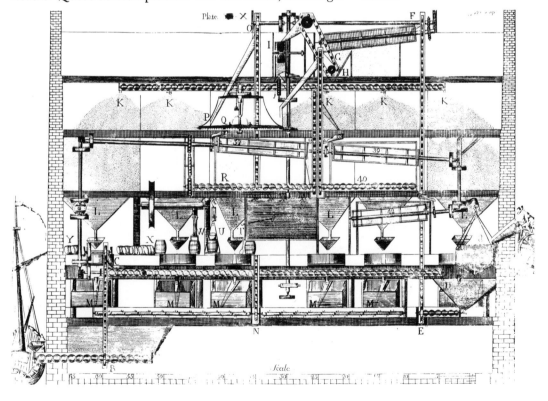

if a member of the congregation had something to say to the assembly, he or she was welcome to do so.

The Friends' adherence to Fox's principles of brotherhood and goodwill prompted them to become social reformers promoting pacifism in England and abroad. For this and other reasons, they were often persecuted—in England, where they refused to attend or fund the Anglican church because they felt it was an inappropriate institution, and in the colonies, where they aroused suspicion and animosity because they refused to take part in the French and Indian War. Nevertheless, the Friends continued to promote pacificism and brotherly love, and by the late 1700s the Society of Friends had not only forbidden slaveholding by its members but had become one of the colonies' loudest voices against slavery. Eventually, the Quaker influence gave rise to other antislavery groups.

Banneker's first formal contact with the Ellicotts came shortly after construction of the mill began. The Ellicotts, wanting to provide for their many workmen, offered to buy supplies from the Banneker farm until their own land began to flourish. Banneker's mother took care of the arrangements and usually delivered the supplies.

After the Ellicotts built their mill and residences, a country store, Ellicott & Co., was erected to supply what was rapidly turning into a thriving community. The store, which carried general supplies, also offered a wide selection of fabrics, including linen, silk, satin, and brocade, that came from all over the world. It soon became a popular meeting place, and Banneker was among those who stopped there to read the newspapers and converse with neighbors.

Banneker especially enjoyed trying to solve mathematical puzzles, which were often posed to him by people he befriended at the store. A typical problem, recorded in his journal, was: "Suppose ladder 60 feet

Founder of the Society of Friends, a religious body whose members are also called Quakers, George Fox began preaching in England in 1647 that Christianity should stress the inner life rather than rituals. His message of contemplation, pacifism, and brotherly love spread to the New World a dozen years later and was adopted by many of the people whom Banneker knew.

long be place in a Street so as to reach a window on the one Side 37 feet high, and without moving it at bottom, will reach another window on the other side of the Street which is 23 feet high, requiring the breadth of the Street."

But what fascinated Banneker most of all were the store's proprietors, the Ellicotts. In the ensuing years, he made the acquaintance of most of the El-

licotts, including Joseph, who in 1774 had withdrawn from the family firm at the Lower Mills to run his own milling operation. He subsequently built a large manor for his family at Ellicott's Upper Mills. An accomplished clockmaker who had heard about Banneker's striking clock, he invited Banneker to his manor to see a timepiece he had made: an eight-foot-high case clock with four faces.

Religious services held by the Society of Friends have always consisted chiefly of quiet contemplation, although congregation members are permitted to address the assembly if they are so inclined. Banneker often attended such services at the Elkridge Meeting House but never joined the Society of Friends.

Ellicott's Lower Mills grew rapidly in the 1770s. This lithograph depicts the homes of George Ellicott (right) and his brothers John (left) and Jonathan (center).

George Ellicott, the son of Andrew Ellicott III (who was the second oldest of the founding brothers), wound up having the greatest impact on Banneker. In 1778, George, who was then 18 years old, was assigned the task of surveying the land for a road linking the mill to Baltimore. The Ellicotts were accustomed to placing responsibility in young hands, having built their first mill in Pennsylvania before Joseph, the oldest brother, had reached the age of 22.

George made accurate topographical maps, plotted the simplest route among the obstacles in the wild landscape, and directed the workers in clearing the

land and grading the roadway. Banneker attentively watched the construction of the road and became acquainted with the young surveyor. Before long, George began visiting Banneker at his cabin.

The two men became fast friends despite the differences in their color and age. They shared not only an interest in the science of mechanics but found that their thinking coincided on a number of topics. Above all, the simplicity of Banneker's life appealed to the Quaker in George, who lent his older friend surveying tools and some books on the subject.

It was the first of several significant gestures that the Ellicotts would make toward Banneker.

5

A CAPITAL
VENTURE

ON APRIL 28, 1788, five years after the end of the revolutionary war, Maryland became the seventh state to join the new union of the United States of America. Although troops from Maryland distinguished themselves in battle during the colonies' fight for independence from England, none of the skirmishes took place within Maryland's borders. As a result, the Revolution barely touched the lives of the people along the upper Patapsco River, where Banneker resided.

By the late 1780s, Banneker's mother had died, leaving him to take care of the family farm by himself. Like other farmers in the area, he quickly saw the advantage in cultivating grain and selling it to the Ellicotts, who ground it at their mill. Consequently, he began to devote a greater portion of his acreage to crops other than tobacco. In his spare time, he made use of the platform telescope and the drafting instruments that George Ellicott had lent him in the fall of 1788.

A free black at a time when more than 100,000 slaves resided in the newly formed state of Maryland, Banneker became an amateur astronomer in 1788. Shortly thereafter, he joined a survey of the land that was to become the District of Columbia, the young nation's new capital.

The passing years had brought added responsibilities to Ellicott, too. More and more, he had become his clan's chief representative at business negotiations in other cities. He was also busy surveying sites far from home. On top of all that, he was about to marry a young woman named Elizabeth

Brooke and was in the midst of constructing their future residence next to his brother Jonathan's house at Ellicott's Lower Mills.

By 1790, Ellicott's young wife had heard a great deal about Banneker from her husband. One day, she and several other people went to see Banneker at his cabin, anxious to meet the free black whom her husband held in such high regard. Years later, their daughter, Martha Tyson, recounted the visit her mother made in *Banneker, the Afric-American Astronomer*:

> [Banneker's] door stood wide open, and so closely was his mind engaged that they entered without being seen. Immediately upon observing them he arose and with much courtesy invited them to be seated. The large oval table at which Banneker sat was strewn with works on astronomy and with scientific appurtenances. He alluded to his love of the study of astronomy and mathematics as quite unsuited to a man of his class, and regretted his slow advancement in them, owing to the laborious nature of his agricultural engagements, which obliged him to spend the greater portion of his time in the fields.

As Banneker himself was quick to admit, his interest in astronomy caused his farm to suffer noticeably. Nevertheless, he continued to concentrate on calculating his first ephemerides, much to George Ellicott's delight.

Finally, in the fall of 1790, Banneker announced that he had finished the project. He was understandably proud of his work and, believing it worthy of publication, sent it to William Goddard at Goddard & Angell, the most prestigious printer in Baltimore. Not only did Goddard reject the manuscript, but so did a second publisher. The printer John Hayes became the third person to reject Banneker's almanac.

A discouraged Banneker then approached George Ellicott for help in getting his work published. Yet it was the young surveyor's cousin Major Andrew Ellicott IV (the son of Joseph Ellicott, the founder of

Major Andrew Ellicott (above), an almanac maker and a cousin of Banneker's close friend and neighbor George Ellicott, checked the accuracy of Banneker's first set of ephemerides. The major was also one of the leading surveyors in the nation. When he was asked to head a survey for a federal capital in 1791, he invited Banneker to serve as his assistant on the project.

Ellicott's Upper Mills) who actually helped Banneker find a printer. Hayes had sent a copy of Banneker's ephemerides to the major, who was carrying out a surveying project in New York, and asked him to verify the accuracy of Banneker's figures. When Andrew Ellicott returned to his home in Philadelphia, he contacted his friend James Pemberton, who was president of the Pennsylvania Society for the Abolition of Slavery, and told him about Banneker's almanac.

Pemberton was very excited by the news. Eager to have at his disposal as much ammunition as possible in the fight against slavery, he was on the lookout for works such as Banneker's. Pemberton knew that if he could help publish an almanac authored by a free black, it would become a valuable weapon in championing the abolitionist cause, serving as proof of the intellectual capabilities of the "Negro given sufficient opportunity."

Pemberton immediately wrote to Joseph Townsend, the president of the Maryland Society for Promoting the Abolition of Slavery, and asked him if he had ever heard of Banneker. Townsend said he had not. But when he asked other members of his society if they knew of Banneker, he found two people who did. One of them was the printer John Hayes; the other was Elias Ellicott, another of George's brothers. Both men were willing to vouch that Banneker was a more than capable astronomer.

The abolitionist societies of Maryland and Pennsylvania became eager to capitalize on the publicity that the printing of an almanac by Banneker would generate. But it was already too late in the year to publish Banneker's set of tables. They decided to direct their energies toward publishing an almanac by Banneker the following year.

In the meantime, another opportunity came Banneker's way. On January 24, 1791, U.S. president

The first president of the United States, George Washington (standing) was an experienced surveyor who gave Andrew Elli-cott detailed instructions on laying out the federal territory.

George Washington appointed a commission of three congressmen to supervise the execution of an important new project: surveying a portion of land, allotted by Maryland and Virginia, to serve as the nation's capital. A new seat of government was needed because Philadelphia, the site of the first Continental Congresses, was not a central location within the new union.

Although Washington asked others to take charge of the matter, he became quite involved in the project. An experienced surveyor himself, he selected Major Andrew Ellicott IV, a rotund man who was not quite 40 years old, to head the surveying team and asked that the work proceed as speedily as possible.

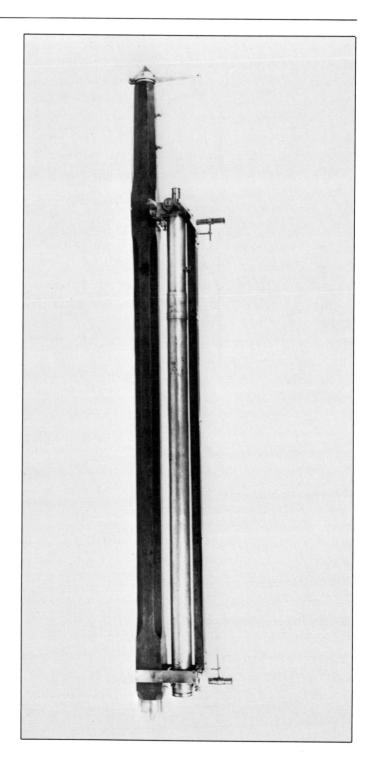

Andrew Ellicott's six-foot-long ze-nith sector, one of two such in-struments employed by Banneker in his survey work. A zenith sec-tor helps a surveyor determine the latitude of specific points on the ground.

The president had given Ellicott little opportunity to assemble an experienced crew. The major felt that 20 well-qualified men should be joining him on the expedition. He had to settle, however, for six men with little or no experience.

One of the first people Ellicott asked to join his surveying team was his cousin George. But George declined the offer—he had too many business commitments. He then suggested that his cousin select Banneker for the position.

Having reviewed Banneker's first set of ephemerides, Andrew Ellicott was already acquainted with the black astronomer's work. The major knew Banneker had the aptitude to handle the task. However, Banneker was about to turn 60 years old, and the rigors of the field might prove difficult for him. But when George gave Banneker a glowing recommendation, Andrew agreed to let him join the team.

Banneker quickly made arrangements with his sisters, who still lived in the area with their respective families, to look after his farm during his absence. Then he consulted Elizabeth Ellicott on what kinds of clothing to bring along, for he was to meet with the people who helped plan the commission but was unaccustomed to sharing the company of those whom George Ellicott's wife called "the most eminent men of the country." Prior to this expedition, Banneker had never been further from his home than a dozen or so miles.

In early February 1791, less than two weeks after Washington's official proclamation of the start of the survey, Banneker and Ellicott left on horseback for Alexandria, Virginia, the initial base of the survey. On the night of February 7, they checked in at Wise's Fountain Tavern in Alexandria. While Ellicott purchased equipment and made the final arrangements for their expedition, Banneker roamed the nearby streets and harbor district, exploring the largest town he had ever seen.

Several days later, the survey team established its base camp near Georgetown, on the Potomac River. This was the site that had been chosen by President Washington to serve as the nation's capital. He had scouted it himself.

Ellicott had been instructed by Secretary of State Thomas Jefferson to lay out the boundaries for the federal territory so that they formed a 10-mile square and included as much interesting landscape as possible. The orders were quite specific. "You are desired to proceed by the first stage to the Federal territory on the Potomac, for the purpose of making a survey of it," Jefferson said. "The first object will be to run the two first lines." After determining the longitude and latitude of the site, the surveyors were to establish the four boundaries for the square and chart the course of the waterways inside the future capital.

The site was favorable for several reasons. It was located between the northern and southern states—an important consideration given the regionalism that plagued the new confederation of states. In addition, the area was accessible by water. The nearby city of Georgetown was already well established as a port and trading center, and Alexandria, one of the busiest ports in the young country, was just a few miles down the Potomac. The new capital district was therefore in a perfect location for economic development. Moreover, a good port in early America was crucial not only to trade but to swift communication.

Wilderness greeted the surveying team and its packhorses when they arrived at the site. Indeed, the capital city's future as a political and economic center must have seemed very distant to its surveyors. Ellicott, as was his custom, chose the highest point in the area for the position of his base camp and set up

Banneker also used this equal-altitude telescope, owned by Andrew Ellicott, to mark off straight boundaries during the survey.

an observatory tent. By making his initial sightings at the highest point of the territory, he helped to ensure the accuracy of all the calculations.

Among the instruments Ellicott used for his observations were two zenith sectors, one of which was almost six feet long. They helped him pinpoint the positions of the stars and thus enabled him to determine the latitude of various positions on the ground. He also used a transit and an equal-altitude instrument, which helped him mark off straight boundaries.

An astronomical clock was another important piece of equipment that the surveying team used. The precise time that each survey of the heavens took place had to be recorded, and an astronomical clock was employed to determine the exact time of the sighting. Ellicott cut down a tree and used the stump, planed as carefully as possible, as a stand for the timepiece, which he enclosed in a wooden case.

One of Banneker's chief tasks was to maintain the astronomical clock. He had to wind it and make sure it kept time at a constant rate. Because it was such a delicate instrument, the clock could prove finicky. As a result, Banneker constantly had to check the temperature of the air surrounding the clock to make sure that the clock's mechanisms were not affected by the cold weather. Even subtle vibrations could hamper the clock's precision.

Under ordinary circumstances, Ellicott preferred to supervise a survey from his base camp, letting others do the fieldwork while he handled the astronomical observations and calculations himself. For this survey, however, he left these tasks, which were physically less demanding than fieldwork, to Banneker and supervised the men in the field. It was an ideal arrangement for Banneker, who enjoyed working with Ellicott's equipment—reputed to be the finest in the country—and kept extensive notes on his astronomical observations.

Yet it was not easy work. Banneker's duties required his constant attention, and his health began to suffer because he followed such a demanding schedule. Because he had to make observations throughout the night, he got little sleep. Living in an observation tent wore on him as well. The weather, often cold and wet, also contributed to his discomfort.

At one point during the survey, President Washington came to the site. He took up lodgings at Suter's Tavern in Georgetown and met with Ellicott. It is not known whether Banneker accompanied the major to this conference. However, Ellicott often invited Banneker to attend briefings with the project's commissioners, so it is possible that a meeting between the president and Banneker actually took place.

Whenever Banneker had a few free moments from his survey work, he turned his attention to the ephemerides that Pemberton and others from the Pennsylvania and Maryland abolition societies had

In the early 1790s, U.S. president George Washington lodged at Suter's Tavern in Georgetown and visited the site of the federal territory. It is likely that Banneker met the president when Andrew Ellicott attended a conference with the head of state at the inn.

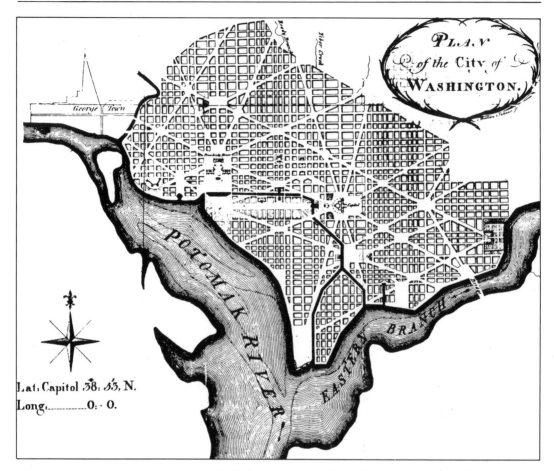

An early plan of the city of Washington in the District of Columbia. This sketch, based on a drawing by the engineer Major Pierre Charles L'Enfant, was published in a 1792 almanac.

asked him to calculate. Because the work Banneker was doing for Ellicott was very complex, his scientific skills soon improved dramatically and made the figuring of an ephemeris a relatively easy task. Still, calculating an ephemeris required time and care—more than he was able to expend while performing survey work.

Finally, by late April, Banneker found himself facing a difficult decision. With the initial phase of the survey having been completed—the four cornerstones of the city had been laid—two matters were prompting him to think about returning home. First, there was his farm. His sisters had been kind enough to oversee it. But now, with the planting season fast approaching, he was needed to help out at home. And then there was his almanac. If he wanted to have it published, he had to return to Baltimore County. Banneker elected to tell Ellicott of his wish to leave the survey.

The project, minus Banneker, continued for several more years. Although two of Ellicott's brothers joined the crew, it remained understaffed. Other problems plagued the project as well. Major Pierre Charles L'Enfant, a French soldier who had fought in the revolutionary war, was commissioned by Thomas Jefferson to execute drawings of the site and submit his plans for laying out the new capital city. A battle of egos soon developed between Andrew Ellicott and L'Enfant, who was eventually relieved of his duties.

The boundary survey for the area, which was called the District of Columbia, was finally completed on January 1, 1793. The federal government moved there seven years later, and the city in the heart of this district, Washington, D.C., has served as the nation's capital ever since. ❧

VIth Month, J U N E, hath 30 Days.

D.H.M.			
Full ○	4	7 55	aft.
Last Q.	11	1 10	aft.
New ●	19	7 49	mo.
First Q.	27	5 10	mo.

☊ { 1 30, 11 ♍ 29, 21 29 } deg.

Planets Places.

D.	☉	♄	♃	♂	♀	☿	☽'s L.
	♊	♈	♎	♍	♉	♉	
1	11	28	22	24	24	19	N. 2
7	17	29	2	26	♊ 1	25	N. 5
13	23	♉ 0	22	29	8	♊ 0	S. 2
19	29	1	22	♎ 0	16	9	S. 5
25	♋ 4	1	22	2	24	17	S. 1

M D	W D	Remarkable days, aspects, weather, &c.	☉ rises	☉ sets	☽'s Pla.	☽ sets.	☽ south	☽ A
1	6	△ ♂ ♀ *Sultry*	4 43	7 17	♎ 27	2 23	9 28	12
2	7	*and*	4 42	7 18	♏ 11	2 57	10 20	13
3	G	Trinity Sund. *dry,*	4 42	7 18	25	3 39	11 17	14
4	2	*close*	4 41	7 19	♐ 9	rises.	Morn.	15
5	3	Spica ♍ sets 1, 47.	4 41	7 19	24	8 18	0 16	16
6	4	*weather,*	4 41	7 19	♑ 9	9 17	1 15	17
7	5	*followed by*	4 40	7 20	23	10 12	2 14	18
8	6	△ ♂ ☿ *thunder*	4 40	7 20	♒ 8	10 56	3 12	19
9	7	*and rain.*	4 40	7 20	23	11 40	4 8	20
10	G	1st Sun. aft. Trin.	4 39	7 21	♓ 7	Morn.	5 2	21
11	2	St. Barnabas. *Cool*	4 39	7 21	21	0 18	5 54	22
12	3	△ ☉ ♃ *breezes,*	4 39	7 21	♈ 4	0 49	6 42	23
13	4	☿ gr. elong. *with*	4 39	7 21	17	1 23	7 30	24
14	5	*flying*	4 39	7 21	♉ 0	2 1	8 18	25
15	6	Pegasi M. r. 10, 32.	4 38	7 22	13	2 35	9 6	26
16	7	[Alban.	4 38	7 22	25	3 8	9 53	27
17	G	2d S. aft. Trin. St.	4 38	7 22	♊ 8	3 48	10 40	28
18	2	*clouds.*	4 38	7 22	20	4 27	11 27	29
19	3	Day's l. 14h. 44m.	4 38	7 22	♋ 1	sets.	Af. 14	●
20	4	☉ en. ♋ *Clear and*	4 38	7 22	13	7 58	0 55	1
21	5	Longest day. *warm.*	4 38	7 22	25	8 40	1 44	2
22	6	*Very*	4 38	7 22	♌ 7	9 30	2 38	3
23	7	△ ♃ ♀ [John Bap.	4 38	7 22	19	10 6	3 25	4
24	G	3d S. aft. Trin. St.	4 38	7 22	♍ 1	10 36	4 5	5
25	2	*sultry.*	4 38	7 22	14	11 7	4 50	6
26	3	*Clear*	4 38	7 22	26	11 41	5 34	7
27	4	♃ sets 1, 2. *and hot*	4 38	7 22	♎ 9	Morn.	6 22	8
28	5	*weather.*	4 38	7 22	23	0 12	7 12	9
29	6	St. Peter and Paul.	4 39	7 21	♏ 6	0 48	8 3	10
30	7	Day's de. 2m. *Rain.*	3 39	7 21	20	1 22	8 58	11

New-Jersey relinquished by the Dutch, and granted to the Duke of York, 1647; settled, 1682; proprietary-government surrendered, 1702.

6

"THE
FIRST
PERFORMANCE"

————— ✿ —————

T HE VARIOUS DUTIES that Banneker performed as a surveyor helped him realize that he was
a more than capable astronomer. Upon returning
from the federal territory in April 1791, he wasted
little time in finishing the calculations for the ephemerides he planned to publish in a 1792 almanac.
Although he felt a bit weak from his three-month
stint with Andrew Ellicott, he was glad to be home
and working with his own telescope.

After months of drawing up charts for Ellicott,
Banneker had come to realize the need for an orderly
presentation of his findings. Consequently, he purchased a volume consisting of 300 blank pages from
the Ellicott & Co. store. The journal was expensive,
but he felt it would soon pay dividends.

By this time, Banneker was accustomed to keeping late hours, so he often scribbled his preliminary
figures onto scratch sheets by candlelight. After reck-
oning the calendar, he figured out the times of sunrise
and sunset, moonrise and moonset, and the rising
and setting of the brightest stars in the sky. He also
determined the times of eclipses—a procedure that
required him to make almost 70 separate calculations
for each eclipse. When he completed the math work,
he always checked over his figures before copying
them into his journal.

*A page from the journal that
Banneker purchased from the Ellicott & Co. store, showing his astronomical calculations for June
1792. Among the entries are the
dates that various phases of the
moon occur, daily weather predic-
tions, and the times that the sun
and moon rise and set.*

Banneker was finished with all the tables by June. His next step was to send the ephemerides to a Georgetown printer, who showed some interest in them but elected not to publish the work. His confidence unshaken, Banneker soon submitted his ephemerides to another printer, William Goddard— a renowned Philadelphia publisher and the same man who had rejected Banneker's first almanac.

This time, however, the results were different. Goddard had recently stopped printing almanacs. But he recognized the potential sales of an almanac by a black author and readily paid Banneker for his work.

Banneker then sought out several more publishers for his ephemerides. In an age when most books did not receive widespread distribution, almanacs were often printed in several cities, by different publishers, with each company issuing its own edition of the text. Thus, by selling a book to several outfits, an author sometimes gained a large readership.

Banneker's quest for additional publishers eventually brought his work before the Maryland and Pennsylvania abolitionist societies, both of which had shown an interest in his ephemerides the previous year. George Ellicott helped him get in touch with the two organizations by sending a letter to his brother Elias, a member of the Pennsylvania Society for the Abolition of Slavery. The letter announced the completion of Banneker's latest set of ephemerides.

Elias worked hard on Banneker's behalf, contacting printers and fellow members of the Pennsylvania abolition society. He also sent a letter to the society's president, James Pemberton, commending Banneker as a man of "strong Natural parts" who "by his own Study hath made himself well Acquainted with the Mathematicks." Elias also reminded Pemberton of the ephemerides that Banneker had previously calculated, "the first performance of the kind ever done by One of his Complection." Elias argued that the publication of an almanac by Banneker would help in "Promoting the Cause of Hummanity as many are of Opinion that the Blacks are Void of Mental endowments."

Pemberton wrote back from Philadelphia that he was eager to help Banneker find an additional publisher. In the meantime, he said, Banneker should transcribe a second copy of his work.

By the time Pemberton's response reached Elias, Banneker had fallen ill and was bedridden. But the news of Pemberton's enthusiasm worked like an elixir on the 60-year-old astronomer. He promptly overcame his illness and managed to make the copy in a few days. He then gave it to George Ellicott, who passed it on to John Todd, a businessman who served as secretary of the Pennsylvania abolition society.

James Pemberton (left) succeeded Benjamin Franklin in 1790 as president of the Pennsylvania Society for the Abolition of Slavery. Shortly thereafter, Pemberton became the first person to use Banneker's scientific work as propaganda in the fight against slavery.

When Todd went on a business trip to Philadelphia, he delivered the package to Pemberton. Shortly thereafter, Pennsylvania's antislavery activists took the necessary steps to arrange for the publication of the almanac.

Meanwhile, Dr. George Buchanan, an influential member of the Maryland Society for Promoting the Abolition of Slavery, gave a speech at an abolition convention on July 4, 1791, in Baltimore. During his address, the physician told the crowd about blacks of exceptional achievement: "Witness Ignacio Sanchez, whose letters are admired by all men of taste; Phillis Wheatley, who distinguished herself as a poetess; the Physician of New Orleans; the Virginia Calculator;

Banneker, the Maryland Astronomer, and many others."

As word of Banneker's accomplishments began to spread, the effort to get his ephemerides printed in Philadelphia gained increasing momentum. Pemberton sent Banneker's calculations to David Rittenhouse, head of the American Philosophical Society (an organization for scholars and thinkers), who verified the accuracy of Banneker's work and called it an extraordinary performance. "Every Instance of Genius amongst the Negroes is worthy of attention," Rittenhouse added, "because their oppressors seem to lay great stress on their supposed inferior mental abilities."

A hub of the abolitionist movement in the 18th century, Philadelphia was the home of Banneker's staunchest supporters during the years when he sought to publish an almanac. Joseph Crukshank, a Philadelphia printer, was one of the first to agree to publish Banneker's scientific work.

Brought to the American colonies as a slave, in 1773 Phillis Wheatley published a poetry collection that won international acclaim and earned her the title of first black American poet. Her writings, like Banneker's scientific work, were published by a printer named Joseph Crukshank, who used them in the fight against slavery as examples of black achievement.

Pemberton solicited a second opinion on Banneker's ephemerides from William Waring, author of the highly popular *Poor Will's Almanac*. He, too, applauded Banneker's efforts, thus setting the stage for Pemberton to approach Joseph Crukshank, a Philadelphia publisher who printed pamphlets for the Society of Friends and was a leading member of the abolitionist movement. Five years earlier, Crukshank had issued the first edition of a collection of poems by Phillis Wheatley, America's first black poet.

As Banneker waited to hear whether or not Crukshank was interested in publishing the 1792 almanac, he began to have second thoughts about the growing interest in his work. His endeavors were gaining the attention of businessmen and political activists not because they admired his scientific skills but because he was black. Yet the reason why he worked hard on the almanac night after night was not to make any sort of political statement. Banneker's romance with the stars was a special relationship, and his findings were remarkable because the sky itself was extraordinary—not because his skin was a dark color.

Banneker considered the situation at some length and decided to cast his objections aside. If he was to become a symbol of black achievement, so be it. The important thing was to make his almanac available to the public.

Benjamin Banneker's
PENNSYLVANIA, DELAWARE,
MARYLAND and VIRGINIA

Almanack

AND
EPHEMERIS
FOR THE YEAR OF OUR LORD
1792

Being BISSEXTILE, or LEAP-YEAR, and the
TENTH YEAR of AMERICAN INDEPENDENCE,
which commenced July 4, 1776.

CONTAINING, the Motions of the Sun and Moon, the true
Places and Aspects of the Planets, the Rising and Setting of
the Sun, and the Rising, Setting and Southing, Place and Age
of the Moon, &c.—The Lunations, Conjunctions, Eclipses,
Judgment of the Weather, Festivals, and other remarkable
Days; Days for holding the Supreme and Circuit Courts of the
United States, as also the usual Courts in Pennsylvania, Delaware, Maryland, and Virginia. Also, several useful Tables,
and valuable Receipts.—Various Selections from the Commonplace-Book of the Kentucky Philosopher, an American Sage;
with interesting and entertaining Essays, in Prose and Verse—
the whole comprising a greater, more pleasing, and useful Variety, than any Work of the Kind and Price in North-America.

BALTIMORE: Printed and Sold, Wholesale and Retail, by
WILLIAM GODDARD and JAMES ANGELL, at their Print-
ing-Office in Market-Street.—Sold, also, by Mr. Joseph
CRUKSHANK, Printer, in Market-Street, and Mr. DANIEL
HUMPHREYS, Printer, in South-Front-Street, Philadelphia;
and by Messrs. HANSON and BOND, Printers, in Alexandria.

7

"FRESH PROOF"

I SOON BECAME apparent that Banneker was not averse to promoting his scientific work. In the middle of August 1791, he carefully composed a long letter that attacked slavery and sent it with a copy of his ephemerides to Secretary of State Thomas Jefferson, one of the most influential figures in the new federal government and an occasional friend of slave owners. Abolitionists had long sought to gain the secretary of state's support, knowing that his backing would lend great weight to their movement.

It is unclear whether the letter was Banneker's idea or was prompted by abolitionists who urged him to capitalize on what was to be an unprecedented publishing event. In fact, there is little in his life either before or after this incident to predict such a public stance. Banneker was a retiring man who had learned from his family that reserve was both a virtue and a necessity for survival. By all accounts, he was as humble as he was grateful for his station as a free black and landowner.

The title page of Banneker's 1792 almanac, originally published in Baltimore by Goddard & Angell.

However, Banneker's father and grandfather had been slaves, and he did not forget this point when writing to the man who had helped shape the Declaration of Independence. He told Jefferson:

I suppose it is a truth too well attested to you, to need a proof here, that we are a race of Beings who have long laboured under the abuse and censure of the world, that we have long been looked upon with an eye of contempt, and that we have long been considered rather as brutish than human, and Scarcely capable of mental endowments. . . . I apprehend you will readily embrace every opportunity to eradicate that train of absurd and false ideas and oppinions which so generally prevail with respect to us, and that your Sentiments are concurrent with mine.

Banneker then pointed out in his letter that before the American Revolution, Jefferson was also in "a State of Servitude":

Here, Sir, was a time in which your tender feelings for your selves engaged you thus to declare, you were then impressed with proper ideas of the great valuation of liberty, and the free possession of those blessings to which you were entitled by nature; but Sir how pitiable is it to reflect, that altho you were so fully convinced of the benevolence of the Father of mankind, and of his equal and impartial distribution of those rights and privileges which he had conferred upon them, that you should at the Same time counteract his mercies, in detaining by fraud and violence so numerous a part of my brethren under groaning captivity and cruel oppression, that you should at the Same time be found guilty of that most criminal act, which you professedly detested in others, with respect to yourselves.

Throughout his life, Jefferson had displayed a great deal of inconsistency regarding the issue of slavery. He had written at one point that he was a reluctant defender of slavery but felt obliged to enforce the wishes of those he represented (his constituency at that time consisted primarily of slaveholders). Nevertheless, he owned slaves and failed to make provisions in his will for their freedom. He was also alleged to have fathered children with slaves, yet these illegitimate offspring remained slaves long after his death. Accordingly, his response to Banneker at the end of August 1791 was difficult to gauge:

SIR, I Thank you sincerely for your letter of the 19th instant and for the Almanac it contained. No body wishes more than I do to see such proofs as you exhibit, that nature has given to our black brethren, talents equal to those of the other colors of men, and that the appearance of a want of them is owing merely to the degraded condition of their existence, both in Africa & America. I can add with truth, that no body wishes more ardently to see a good system commenced for raising the condition both of their body & mind to what it ought to be, as fast as the imbecility of their present existence, and other circumstances which cannot be neglected, will admit.

I have taken the liberty of sending your Almanac to Monsieur de Condorcet, Secretary of the Academy of Sciences at Paris, and member of the Philanthropic society, because I considered it as a document to which your whole colour had a right for their justification against the doubts which have been entertained of them.

The Marquis de Condorcet was a leading French intellectual, mathematician, and philosopher. He was also a revolutionary who supported the new French republic, which was patterned after the United States. It is likely that Jefferson sent the almanac to Condorcet, who helped found France's Society of the Friends of Blacks, not because Jefferson supported black rights but because he was trying to attract favorable attention there. Not the least of Jefferson's motives was his desire to parlay his tenure as secretary of state into a successful bid for the presidency.

While these correspondences were taking place, last-minute problems impeded the publication of Banneker's almanac. William Goddard, claiming that Banneker had sold him exclusive rights to the almanac, refused to deal with Crukshank, Banneker's other printer. Having gotten hold of the only copy of the book's introduction, which was written by Maryland senator James McHenry, Goddard refused to release the book's opening to Banneker's Philadelphia publisher.

Sir
                              Philadelphia Aug. 30. 1791.

    I thank you sincerely for your letter of the 19th. instant and for the Almanac it contained. no body wishes more than I do to see such proofs as you exhibit, that nature has given to our black brethren, talents equal to those of the other colours of men, & that the appearance of a want of them is owing merely to the degraded condition of their existence both in Africa & America. I can add with truth that no body wishes more ardently to see a good system commenced for raising the condition both of their body & mind to what it ought to be, as fast as the imbecillity of their present existence, and other circumstances which cannot be neglected, will admit.   I have taken the liberty of sending your almanac to Monsieur de Condorcet, Secretary of the Academy of sciences at Paris, and member of the Philanthropic society, because I considered it as a document to which your whole colour had a right for their justification against the doubts which have been entertained of them. I am with great esteem, Sir

            Your most obedt. humble servt.

                          Th: Jefferson

Mr. Benjamin Banneker
    near Ellicot's, lower mills. Baltimore county

V.66

In August 1791, Secretary of State Thomas Jefferson (left) received a letter from Banneker requesting that the influential politician "eradicate that train of absurd and false ideas and oppinions which so generally prevail with respect to" blacks. Jefferson's response (opposite), which maintained that "no body wishes more than I do to see such proofs as you exhibit, that nature has given to our black brethren," was featured in the 1793 edition of Banneker's almanac.

Goddard's actions threatened not only to limit the circulation of the almanac but reduce the amount of money Banneker would earn from the book's sales. In addition, Banneker greatly feared the damage that would be done to his reputation if it appeared that he had ineptly managed the negotiations with Goddard. These possibilities compelled Banneker to send a detailed description of his dealings with Goddard to Elias Ellicott, who relayed the information to James Pemberton.

Pemberton wrote immediately to Goddard, appealing to him on Banneker's behalf. "Towards the close of last year, I first Recd. information of the Astronomical Genius of Benj. Banniker a Black man in the neighborhood of Baltimore and that he had made calculations for an Almanac for the pres. t year but he was disappointed in the publication of it. . . . I now only Sollicit thy attentive benevolence to poor Banniker to make further Compensation as thou may Judge to make up in some measure for the disappointment he will be subjected by the publication of his performance being laid aside here."

Pemberton's polite chiding apparently did the trick. "I shall consider it an Act of Justice & Civility to give [Crukshank] the Advantage of selling the Work, & will, therefore, send him a Number of the first Impression," Goddard responded. "I am heartily disposed not only to be just, but generous to poor Benjamin."

Banneker's first almanac went on sale in late December 1791. Goddard advertised the book as "BENJAMIN BANNEKER'S highly approved ALMANACK, for 1792." The 24-page volume was also promoted by the Pennsylvania and Maryland abolition societies.

McHenry's introduction, which sketched Banneker's life from his schoolboy days to the time of his "astronomical researches," helped sell the almanac as well. Banneker's life, the senator wrote, was "fresh proof that the powers of the mind are disconnected with the colour of the skin, or, in other words, a striking contradiction to [the] doctrine, that 'Negroes are naturally inferior to the whites and unsusceptible of attainments in arts and sciences.' In every civilized country we shall find thousands of whites, liberally educated, and who have enjoyed greater opportunities of instruction than this Negro, his inferior in those intellectual acquirements and capacities that form the most characteristic feature in the human race."

The title page of Banneker's first almanac also emphasized his race. It included the following message:

THE
PENNSYLVANIA, DELAWARE
MARYLAND, AND VIRGINIA
ALMANACK,

FOR THE YEAR 1792:

A COMPLETE and ACCURATE EPHEMERIS, calculated by the ingenious Mr. BENJAMIN BANNEKER, a *free black Man*, (a Native of this County, born of *African Parents*) whose Calculations, now offered the Public, have met the Approbation of several of the most distinguished Astronomers in America.

CONTAINING, interesting Particulars of the virtuous Life and laudable Pursuits of BENJAMIN BANNEKER, and his Progress to ASTRONOMIC FAME.—The Motions of the Sun and Moon, the true Places and Aspects of the Planets, the Rising and Setting of the Sun, and the Rising, Setting and Southing, Place and Age of the Moon, &c.—The Lunations, Conjunctions, Eclipses, Judgment of the Weather, Festivals, and other remarkable Days; Days for holding the Supreme and Circuit Courts of the *United States*, as also the usual Courts in *Pennsylvania, Delaware, Maryland, and Virginia.*—Various Selections from the Commonplace-Book of the *Kentucky Philosopher*, an *American Sage*; with interesting and entertaining Essays, in Prose and Verse—the whole comprising a greater, more pleasing, and useful Variety, than any Work of the *Kind* and *Price* in *North-America.*

N. B. The above Work, amongst other Particulars, contains the following Essays, which will be found highly pleasing and instructive :—The Planetary and Terrestrial Worlds, comparatively considered—Remarks on the Swiftness of Time—Origin of the Gray Mare being the better Horse—The Two Bees—On Health—Origin of the Proverb, " *Lay hold of the Tail if you can, and be sure to keep it fast*"—Extracts from the Writings of the Ancients of distinguished Fame—The Stings of Poverty, Disease and Violence, less pungent than those of guilty Passions—The Balance of Happiness equal—Effusions on a Town and Country Life—On Negro Slavery and the Slave-Trade—Also, a List of the Legislature and principal Officers of the General Government.

⁎ *Orders, from our Country and distant Customers, will be duly attended to.*

At a Meeting of the " *Maryland Society for promoting the gradual Abolition of Slavery, and the Relief of free Negroes and others, unlawfully held in Bondage,*" *held in Baltimore, the first Day of October,* 1791,

MESSRS. GODDARD and ANGELL presented to the Society an ALMANACK for the Year 1792, the *Astronomical Calculations* thereof performed by BENJAMIN BANNEKER, *a black Man, a Descendant of African Parents.*—The Calculations appear to be attested by a Number of respectable Characters, as very accurate.

The Society considering the Performance a Work of Merit, worthy their Attention as a Body, agree to patronise the same, and use Endeavours to promote the Sale thereof.

Whereupon Resolved, That the Secretary furnish Messrs. Goddard and Angell with a Copy of the foregoing Determination, to be made public.

Copied, by Direction, and signed,
JOSEPH TOWNSEND, Secretary.

An advertisement for Banneker's 1792 almanac that appeared in the December 2, 1791, issue of the Maryland Journal and Baltimore Advertiser.

A prominent antislavery activist, Maryland senator James McHenry wrote an introduction to the first edition of Banneker's almanac that praised the author's efforts and denounced racial prejudice. "The system that would assign to these degraded blacks an origin different from the whites," McHenry wrote, "if it is not ready to be deserted by philosophers, must be relinquished as similar instances multiply."

The Editors of the PENNSYLVANIA, DELAWARE, MARYLAND, AND VIRGINIA ALMANACK, feel themselves gratified in the Opportunity of presenting to the Public, through the Medium of their Press, what must be considered an extraordinary effort of Genius—a COMPLETE and ACCURATE EPHEMERIS for the year 1792, calculated by a sable Descendant of Africa, who, by this specimen of Ingenuity, evinces, to Demonstration, that mental Powers and Endowments are not the exclusive Excellence of white People, but that the Rays of Science may alike illumine the Minds of Men of every Clime, (however they may differ in the Colour of their Skin) particularly those whom Tyrant-Custom hath too long taught us to depreciate as a Race inferior in intellectual Capacity.

Inside the almanac, besides the ephemerides, were essays: "The Planetary and Terrestrial Worlds," "Remarks on the Swiftness of Time," "Origin of the Gray's Mare being the Better Horse," "Extracts from the Common-Place Book of the Kentucky Philosopher," and a treatise on tree diseases. Toward the end of the 18th century, it had become common practice to include news items and political tracts in an almanac.

The first edition of Banneker's almanac sold out quickly, prompting a second edition to be issued. The book's widespread success had a significant impact on Banneker's life because it freed him from having to do a large amount of farm work. Instead of raising cash crops, he needed only to keep a small garden and take care of his honeybees. As a result, he had much more free time than in the past, and he spent a good deal of it at his worktable.

Banneker also passed the time by playing host to the many people who stopped by his cabin to talk with a new and popular author. A loner for much of his life, he enjoyed such visits, showing his guests the striking clock he had made and the oak table where he worked on his calculations. Indeed, Banneker was amused by the notion that at the age of 61 he had become something of a national celebrity. ❧

Benjamin Bannaker's

PENNSYLVANIA, DELAWARE, MARY-LAND, AND VIRGINIA

ALMANAC,

FOR THE

YEAR of our LORD 1795;

Being the Third after Leap-Year.

BANNAKER.

—PRINTED FOR—

And Sold by JOHN FISHER, *Stationer.*

BALTIMORE.

8

ECLIPSING FAME

BANNEKER'S 1792 ALMANAC was followed by the publication of another almanac the following year. For the most part, the second book had the same format as the first. But there were a couple of notable differences between the two volumes. The 1793 almanac included Banneker's correspondence with Thomas Jefferson as well as "A Plan Of a *Peace Office* for the United States," an essay on pacifism allegedly written by Banneker but most likely penned by antislavery activist Benjamin Rush, a Philadelphia physician.

Banneker's 1793 almanac featured these additions and sold exceedingly well. In fact, it outsold a similar work prepared by Andrew Ellicott. This accomplishment deeply gratified Banneker, who recalled that Ellicott's printer, John Hayes, had rejected the first ephemerides that Banneker had calculated.

Banneker continued to publish almanacs for several more years. His correspondence for 1793 reveals that in addition to calculating the ephemerides for 1794, he also attempted to launch an English edition of his work. Such a book was certainly desirable to British antislavery activists, who read from Banneker's American almanacs in the House of Commons in an attempt to advance the abolitionist cause in England.

This woodcut portrait of Banneker appeared on the cover of several editions of his 1795 almanac.

P R E F A C E.

GENTLE READER,

TO make an *ALMANAC* is not *fo eafy a matter as fome people think—like a well furnifhed table it requires to have a variety of difhes to fuit every palate, befides confiderable fkill in the cooking—Now, as it is impoffible to fuit all the difhes to every particular tafte, we hope you will not be offended: fhould you find any not entirely to your liking as we are certain there are a great many which will fuit you to a hair. We are perfuaded you will not only be entertained but inftructed by our Almanac, for we have ranfacked all the repofitories of learning to cull a few flowers for your amufement. Moreover, Kind Reader, as we believe you would think the better of a man for having a decent coat on his back fo we have exerted ourfelves to make our Almanac appear in a more refpectable drefs, than fome other Almanac mongers have done, who, it would feem, have thought their Almanacs not worthy a good coat*

But there is one difh we invite you to partake of, and we are prouder of it than of all the reft put together; and to whom do you think are we indebted for this part of our entertainment? Why, to a Black Man—Strange! Is a Black capable of compofing an Almanac? Indeed it is no lefs ftrange than true; and a clever wife long headed Black he is: It would be telling fome whites if they had made as much ufe of their great fchool learning, as this fage philofopher has made of the little teaching he has got.

The labours of the juftly celebrated Banneker will likewife furnifh you with a very important leffon, courteous reader, which you will not find in any other Almanac namely, that the Maker of the Univerfe is no refpecter of colours; that the colour of the fkin is no ways connected with ftrength of mind or intellectual powers; that although the God of Nature has marked the face of the African with a darker fhade than his brethren, he has given him a foul equally capable of refinement. To the untutored Blacks the following elegant lines of GRAY may be applied.

" Full many a gem of pureft ray ferene,
" The dark unfathom d caves of ocean bear :
" Full many a flower is borne to blufh unfeen,
" And wafte its fragrance on the defert air."

Nor you ye proud, impute to thefe the fault
If Afric's fons to genius are unknown,
For Banneker has prov'd they may acquire a name
As bright, as lafting as your own.

Pages (right and opposite) from Banneker's 1792 almanac.

An English edition, however, was never produced. Calculating a new set of figures for foreign readers proved too great a strain on the aging Banneker. When an illness jeopardized the production of his American almanac, he decided to abandon his work on the English edition.

The ANATOMY *of* MAN's BODY, *as governed by the Twelve Constellations.*

♈ The Head and Face

♊ Arms

♌ Heart

♎ Reins

♐ Thighs

♒ Legs

♉ Neck

♋ Breast

♍ Bowels

♏ Secrets

♑ Knees

♓ The Feet.

To find where the sign is.
First find the Day of the Month, and against the Day you have the Sign or Place of the Moon in the 6th Column. Then finding the sign there, it shews the Part of the body it governs.

MAN's head and face Heaven's ram obey,
 His neck the neck-strong bull does sway,
The arm-twining twins guides hands and arms;
Breasts, sides and stomach *Cancer* charms,
The lion rules his back and heart,
Bowels and belly's *Virgo* part;
Reins, haunches, navel, *Libra* tends,
Bladder and Secrets *Scorpio* befriends:
The half-hors'd bowman rules the thighs,
And to the kid our knees suffice;
Our legs are but the butler's fees,
The fish our footsteps oversees.

Sales of Banneker's almanac continued to soar in 1794. Indeed, the year marked the zenith of his career as a maker of almanacs. "The Sale of my Almanac for this present Year, has gaven [sic] me encouragement to make a calculation for the ensuing year," he wrote to James Pemberton.

A new feature in Banneker's 1795 almanac appeared on its front cover: a woodcut portrait of the author in typical Quaker dress (even though he never formally joined any religious sect). "The most sensible of those who make scientific researches," he wrote in the book, "is he who believes himself the farthest from the goal, & who whatever advances he has made in his road, studies as if he yet knew nothing and marches as if he were only yet beginning to make his first advance." Despite this claim, the book did not sell as well as past volumes. Nor did the 1796 edition. Finally, in 1797, he published the last of his almanacs, even though he continued to calculate ephemerides for another eight years.

The waning sales of Banneker's almanac were chiefly due to two factors: competition from other almanacs and a steady loss of interest in the abolitionist movement. As the 1790s progressed, the number of almanacs available to the public increased dramatically. Many readers simply elected to buy almanacs other than Banneker's. At the same time, the newly independent United States was turning its attention more and more to other issues besides slavery, thus lessening the demand for publications with abolitionist messages. In fact, the views held by antislavery groups met with a responsive public for only a brief period in the 1790s, and organizations such as the Maryland Society for Promoting the Abolition of Slavery folded shortly after the last edition of Banneker's almanac appeared.

As soon as the clamor surrounding Banneker died down, a change began to occur in his life. When some of his neighbors discovered that he was no longer farming his land, they asked if they could rent portions of it for growing their own crops. Banneker agreed to let them. Yet when it came time for his tenants to pay the rent, he had difficulty in collecting

EXTRACTS FROM THE DEBATES IN THE LAST SESSION OF
THE BRITISH PARLIAMENT, APR. 1792.

*Abstract from the speech of William Pitt, esq. on the motion for
the Abolition of the Slave-Trade.*

THERE are very few of those who have spoken this
night, who have not thought it their duty to declare their
full and entire concurrence with my honorable friend in
promoting the abolition of the slave-trade, as their ulti-
mate object: however we may differ as to the time and
manner of it, *we are agreed in the abolition itself*; and my
honorable friends have expressed their agreement in this
sentiment with that sensibility upon the subject, which
humanity does most undoubtedly require.

The point now in dispute between us is a difference
merely as to the period of time at which the abolition
ought to take place. I therefore congratulate this house,
the country, and the world, that this great point is gained; that we may now consider this trade as having *received
its condemnation*; that its sentence is sealed; that this *curse
of mankind* is seen by the house in its true light; that the
greatest stigma on our national character which ever yet
existed, is about to be removed; and, sir (which is still
more important) *that mankind, I trust, in general, are now
likely to be delivered from the greatest practical evil that ever
has afflicted the human race—from the severest and most extensive calamity recorded in the history of the world.*

Mr. M. Montague. I shall now conclude with repeating
a profession I formerly made—that I never will cease to
promote the abolition of the slave-trade, with every facul-
ty of body and mind, till the injuries of humanity are re-
dressed, and the national character relieved from the deep-
est disgrace that is recorded in the annals of mankind.

Mr. C. J. Fox [in reply to Addington, speaker of the
house.] If the question be, whether Britain shall retain
the slave-trade and the West-India islands, or part with
them both together; I do not hesitate a moment in

*In addition to containing ephe-
merides, almanacs in the 18th
century also featured such news-
worthy items as accounts of recent
events and political tracts. William Pitt, a member of the English Parliament, wrote this essay
on slavery, which was published
in Banneker's 1793 almanac.*

the amount that was due. No longer young and often
in ill health, he lacked the strength to press his neighbors for his money. As the years passed, some of the
tenants not only refused to pay what they owed but
threatened Banneker to prevent him from asking for
his rent.

Eventually, the threats became more and more alarming. On two separate occasions in the late 1790s, people fired gunshots in Banneker's direction. A few years later, his house was robbed. Fortunately, his astronomical instruments were not touched.

Deciding that his property was the cause of his difficulty, Banneker determined to sell portions of it for his own protection. For more than 60 years, the Bannekers had owned the land known as Stout and had worked it for their chief means of support. The 100 acres, it seemed, was proof of their independence. But now the time had come to give it up.

The pain that Banneker felt in selling his family's land was softened somewhat when his nephew Greenbury Morten elected to buy a parcel of 20 acres. The Ellicotts purchased most of the remaining land, including the area on which Banneker's cabin stood. The sales agreement contained a provision that allowed him to reside in the cabin during his final years.

The Ellicotts also agreed to stagger their payments to Banneker so as to give him a steady income for the rest of his life. To figure out the rate of compensation, Banneker put his mathematical skills to work in a bizarre way: He attempted to calculate how many years he had left to live. "I believe I shall live fifteen years," he concluded, "and consider my land worth $1180 Maryland Currency; by receiving $112 a year, for fifteen years I shall in the contemplated time, receive its full value; if on the contrary I die before that day, you will be at liberty to take possession."

Shortly after the sale of the land was formalized in October 1799, Banneker struck a new arrangement with the Ellicotts. They gave him a charge account at the Ellicott & Co. store, and the amount of his purchases was subtracted from the sum that the Ellicotts owed him each year. Always the statistician, Banneker kept track of his purchases in a journal. His records reveal that toward the end of his life he bought what must have immediately become one of his most prized possessions: a pocket watch much like the one he had dissected nearly 40 years earlier.

Apparently, the sale of the land brought Banneker the sense of peace he desired, and during his last years he settled into a routine of light chores and scientific study. When night fell, he often sat at his worktable with his telescope and remained there until dawn, observing the heavens.

One of Banneker's closest friends during the last years of his life was Susanna Mason, a cousin of the Ellicotts. Founder of an association for the relief of Baltimore's poor, she first met the noted maker of almanacs in 1796. They carried out a warm correspondence, with Mason at one point sending Banneker a poem that included the following prediction:

> But thou, a man exalted high,
> Conspicuous in the world's keen eye
> On record now thy name's enrolled,
> And future ages will be told,
> There lived a man called Banneker,
> An African astronomer.

By the early 1800s, Banneker's infirmities had begun to increase, and it became difficult for him to pursue his interest in astronomy. Then, on October 9, 1806, he suddenly felt ill during a Sunday walk and hurried home, accompanied by a friend he had encountered along the way. As soon as Banneker entered his cabin, he collapsed on his couch. He died that same day, one month before his 75th birthday.

Banneker had left instructions for dispersing his personal effects. Several of the items, including his scientific books and instruments as well as his worktable, were bequeathed to George Ellicott. They were quickly carted away. Banneker also passed on to his longtime friend the journal containing his astronomical calculations and his diary. The rest of his possessions went to his sisters.

A funeral service was held for Banneker two days after he died. While the ceremony was taking place, a strange thing happened. As Banneker's body was being lowered into the ground close to his cabin, the wooden building suddenly burst into flames and burned to the ground. When the fire was over, none of its contents remained—not even Banneker's striking clock.

Later that month, the *Federal Gazette and Baltimore Daily Advertiser* gave Banneker a lengthy and laudatory obituary notice—a clear indication of the local community's high regard for him:

> On Sunday, the 9th instant, departed this life at his residence in Baltimore county, in the 73d [sic] year of his age, Mr. BENJAMIN BANNEKER, a black man, and immediate descendant of an African father. He was well known in his neighborhood for his quiet and peaceable demeanor, and among scientific men as an astronomer and mathematician. In early life he was instructed in the most common rules of arithmetic, and thereafter, with the assistance of different authors, he was enabled to acquire a perfect knowledge of all the higher braches of learning. Mr. B was the calculator of several almanacs which were published in this as well as some of the neighboring states, and although of late years none of his almanacs were published, yet he never failed to calculate one every year, and left them among his papers, prefering solitude to mixing with society, and devoted the greatest part of his time in reading and contemplation, and to no books was he more attached than the scriptures. At his decease he bequeathed all his astronomical and philosophical books and paper to a friend.
>
> Mr. Banneker is a prominent instance to prove that a descendant of Africa is susceptible of as great mental improvement and deep knowledge into the mysteries of nature as that of any other nation.

Thirty-nine years later, three historians went looking for Banneker's gravesite. They remarked that "beneath two tulip trees, so grown as to seem one, lay the mortal remains of the black astronomer of Maryland. A few yards to the northwest of the grave

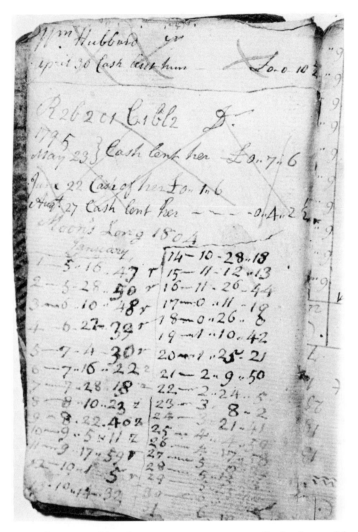

A page from Banneker's common-place book. He kept this diary to record bits of information, including astronomical observations, household finances, and personal thoughts.

was the site of his house, not a vestige of which could then be seen. It was marked only by a shallow cavity, at the southeastern end of which stood a tall Lombardy poplar, said to be that which overshadowed the gable end of his house."

Finally, in 1954, on a spot in Oella, Maryland, that historical records showed to be the location of Banneker's farm, the Maryland Historical Society erected a marker commemorating America's first black man of science. It read

BENJAMIN BANNEKER
1731–1806
SELF-EDUCATED NEGRO
MATHEMATICIAN-ASTRONOMER
HE MADE THE FIRST MARYLAND ALMANAC IN 1792
HIS ACHIEVEMENTS RECOGNIZED
BY THOMAS JEFFERSON
WAS BORN, LIVED HIS ENTIRE LIFE AND
DIED NEAR HERE.

A Banneker commemorative stamp issued by the U.S. Postal Service on February 15, 1980.

In the years that followed, the marker had to be replaced several times because it was vandalized. Efforts to restore it were halted in the late 1960s. Today, the site of Banneker's home is no longer identified to the public.

History, it seems, has been less kind to the modest Banneker than to his militant black contemporaries who helped shape early America. The slave-revolt leaders Denmark Vesey, Gabriel Prosser, and Nat Turner are still widely remembered for their violent attempts to dispel the myth that blacks were content as second-class citizens. Banneker, in contrast, a free black at a time when people of his status were usually ignored by white society, remains far less celebrated. Indeed, his name is more often associated with the fight against slavery than with his illustrious accomplishments as a mathematician and astronomer—scientific achievements that still shine across the ages like rays of light from the brightest of stars. ❧

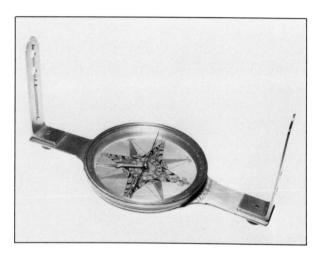

The compass used during the initial survey of the District of Columbia.

CHRONOLOGY

1731	Born Benjamin Banneker on November 9 in the British colony of Maryland
1737	Moves with family to a large tobacco farm in Baltimore County
ca. 1751	Builds a wooden clock
1788	Develops an interest in astronomy after receiving astronomical instruments from his neighbor George Ellicott
1789	Banneker makes his first attempt at calculating a set of ephemerides
1791	Becomes an assistant in the survey of the District of Columbia; corresponds with Secretary of State Thomas Jefferson
1792	Banneker's first almanac is published
1797	The last of his almanacs is published
1806	Banneker dies on October 9 in Baltimore County, Maryland

FURTHER READING

Allen, Will W. *Banneker: The Afro-American Astronomer.* Freeport, NY: Books for Libraries Press, 1971.

Bedini, Silvio A. *The Life of Benjamin Banneker.* New York: Scribners, 1971.

Clark, Margaret Goff. *Benjamin Banneker: Astronomer and Scientist.* Champaign, IL: Garrard, 1971.

Ferris, Jeri. *What Are You Figuring Now? A Story About Benjamin Banneker.* Minneapolis: Carolrhoda, 1988.

Franklin, John Hope. *From Slavery to Freedom: A History of Negro Americans.* New York: Knopf, 1980.

Graham, Shirley. *Your Most Humble Servant: The Story of Benjamin Banneker.* New York: Messner, 1949.

Lewis, Claude. *Benjamin Banneker: The Man Who Saved Washington.* New York: McGraw-Hill, 1970.

Meier, August, and Elliott Rudwick, eds. *The Making of Black America.* New York: Atheneum, 1969.

Patterson, Lillie. *Benjamin Banneker: Genius of Early America.* Nashville: Abingdon Press, 1978.

Sagendorph, Robb. *America and Her Almanacs: Wit, Wisdom & Weather, 1639–1970.* Boston: Little, Brown, 1970.

Wilson, Ruth. *Our Blood and Tears: Black Freedom Fighters.* New York: Putnam, 1972.

INDEX

PICTURE CREDITS

KEVIN CONLEY was born in Detroit, Michigan, and holds a bachelor's degree in theater from Yale University and a master's degree in classics from Wayne State University. He has edited *Empire*, a literary magazine composed of the work of inmates in the New York State prison system, and has written for *Cineaste*, *Metro Times*, *Straits*, and other publications. He currently lives in Brooklyn, New York.

NATHAN IRVIN HUGGINS is W.E.B. Du Bois Professor of History and Director of the W.E.B. Du Bois Institute for Afro-American Research at Harvard University. He previously taught at Columbia University. Professor Huggins is the author of numerous books, including *Black Odyssey: The Afro-American Ordeal in Slavery*, *The Harlem Renaissance*, and *Slave and Citizen: The Life of Frederick Douglass*.